The Five Kingdo

Scientists have placed all living things into five **kingdoms**. The organisms in each group represent one of the five kingdoms of living things.

Label each kingdom.

| animals | fungi | monerans | plants | protists |

l

Family of Living Things

Scientists divide living things into five main groups called **kingdoms**.

Complete the chart comparing the five kingdoms.

	Kingdoms				
	Animal	**Plant**	**Fungi**	**Protists**	**Monerans**
Does it make food? (yes; no; some)					
Does it move about? (yes; no; some)					
How many cells does it have? (one; many)					
Does the cell have a nucleus? (yes; no)					

Name_____

Animal or Plant?

Scientists divide all living things into five groups called **kingdoms**. Two of the largest are the animal kingdom and the plant kingdom.

Compare these two kingdoms by using the chart. Check the correct box or boxes next to each characteristic.

Characteristic	Plant	Animal
all living organisms		
formed from cells		
cells have chlorophyll		
cells have no chlorophyll		
makes its own food		
gets food from outside		
moves from place to place		
has limited movement		
can reproduce its own kind		
depends on the sun's energy		

3

Name_____

The Plant World

This chart shows how scientists group the different kinds of plants in the plant world.

Place a check in the column(s) that represent the plant with that characteristic.

Plants that make seeds		Plants that don't make seeds
Seeds from flowers	**Seeds from cones**	

monocot

dicot

conifer

fungus

fern

moss

algae

	monocot	dicot	conifer	moss	fern	fungus	algae
is green							
makes seeds							
makes seeds in a flower							
makes seeds with two seed parts							
makes seeds with one seed part							
makes seeds in a cone							
produces spores							
has leaves with veins							
has leaves with parallel veins							
has leaves with net-like veins							
has needle-like leaves							
is a one-celled plant							

Plant Parts

Label the parts of a bean plant.

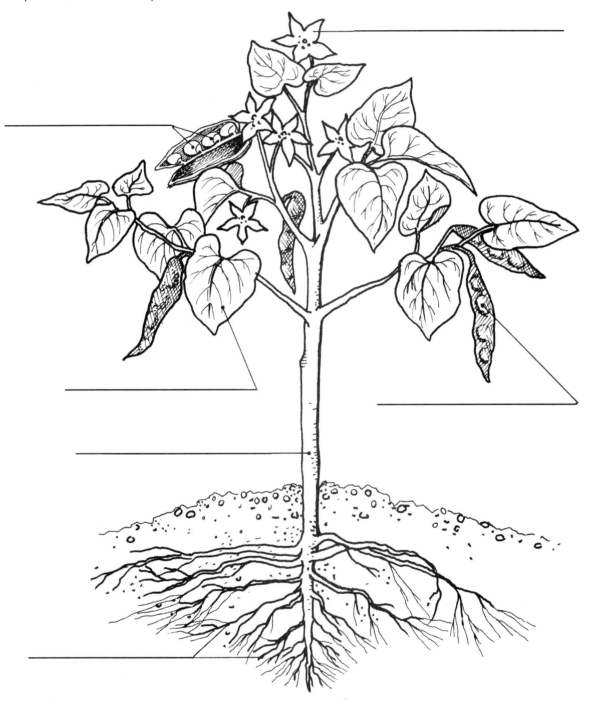

flower	fruit	leaf
root	seeds	stem

A Flowering Plant

Label the parts of a flowering plant.

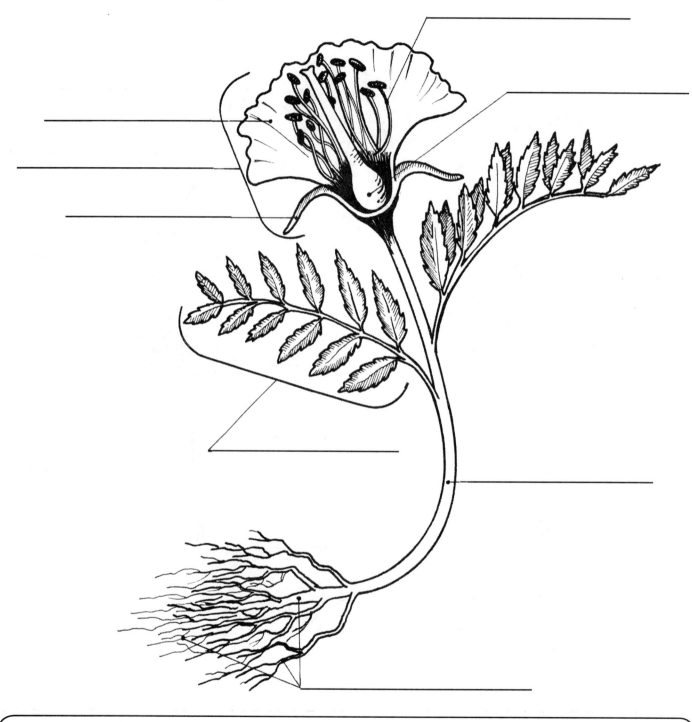

flower	leaf	petal
pistil	roots	sepal
stem	stamen	

Flower Parts

Label the parts of the two flowers. Some words may be used more than once.

| ovary | petal | pistil | sepal | stamen |

Seed-Producing Parts of a Flower

Label the seed-producting parts of a flower.

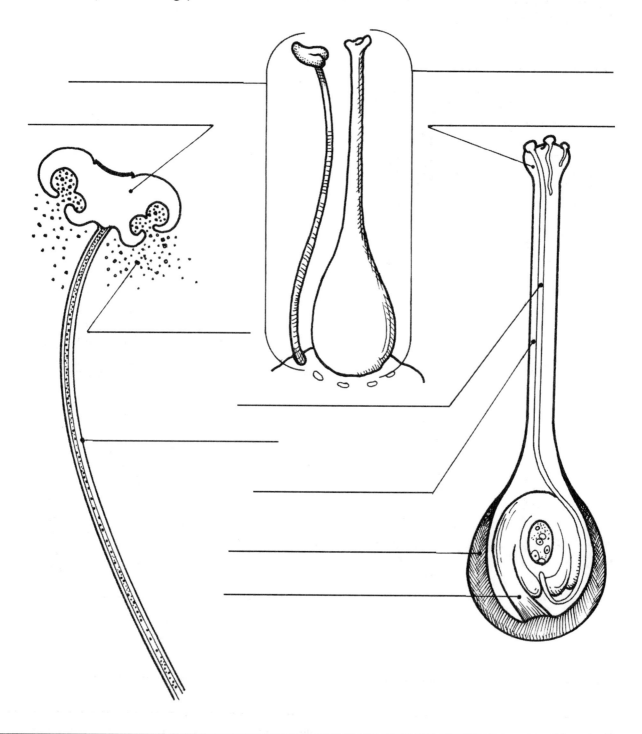

anther	filament	ovary	ovule	pistil
pollen grains	pollen tube	stamen	stigma	style

Pollination

Label the main parts involved in each type of pollination.

anther	cross-pollination	ovary
pistil	pollen grains	self-pollination
stamen	stigma	style

Monocot or Dicot?

Describe the characteristic that makes each plant either a dicot or a monocot. Label each plant part either *dicot* or *monocot*.

Seeds

Flowers

_____ _____ _____ _____

_____ _____ _____ _____

Leaves

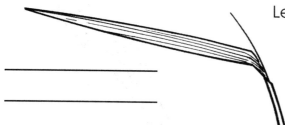 

_____ _____

_____ _____

Vascular bundles
in stem

Roots

_____ _____   _____ _____

_____ _____   _____ _____

bundles in a ring	fibrous	net-veined
one cotyledon	parallel veins	parts in fours or fives
parts in threes	scattered bundles	taproot
two cotyledon		

Eating Plant Parts

Label the edible part of each plant to describe what part of the plant is eaten.

_____ _____

_____ _____ _____

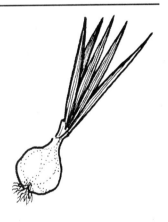

_____ _____ _____

bulb	flower	fruit	leaves
root	seed	stem	tuber

Corn Seed

Label the parts of a corn seed. Some words may be used more than once.

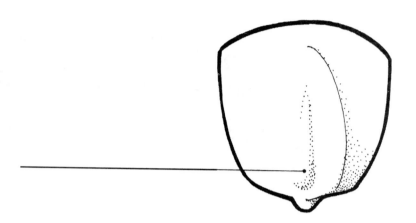

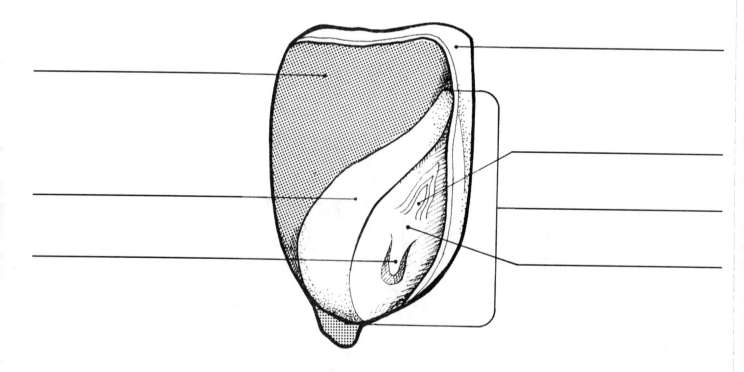

cotyledon (food)	embryo	endosperm
epicotyl (leaves)	hypocotyl (stem)	radicle (root)
seed and fruit coats		

Bean Seed

Label the parts of a bean seed.

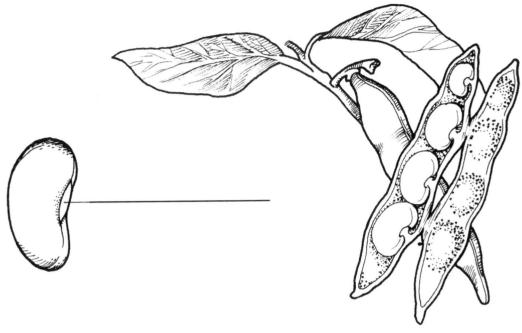

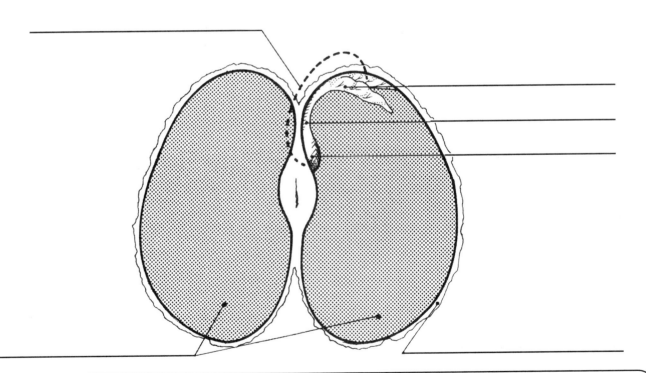

| cotyledon (food) | embryo | epicotyl (leaves) | hilum |
| hypocotyl (stem) | radicle (root) | seed coat | |

Growing Bean Plants

Label the parts of a growing bean plant.

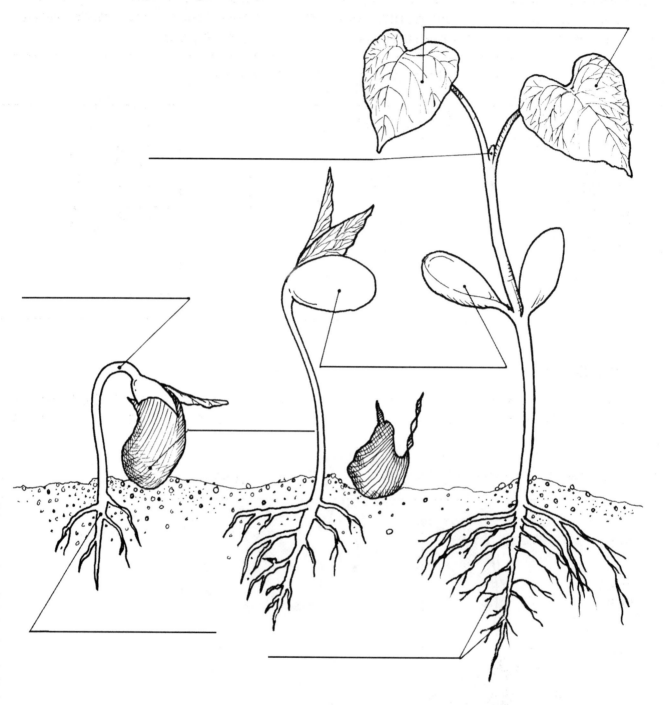

cotyledon	first leaves	hypocotyl (stem)
radicle	roots	seed coat
terminal bud		

Tropisms

Tropisms occur when plants bend in response to outside stimuli such as light, gravity, or water. Three common types are **geotropism**, which is caused by gravity; **phototropism**, which is caused by light; and **hydrotropism**, which is caused by water.

Label the type of tropism affecting the plant in each picture.

_____   _____   _____

Make a Prediction

The flowerpot in the first picture was placed on its side. The plant will continue to receive water and light. How will the plant's growth be affected after three weeks of lying on its side?

Draw a picture of what the plant will look like after three weeks.

Before   Three weeks later

Traveling Seeds

Seeds are dispersed, or scattered, from the parent plant in many ways. The pictures show six examples of how seeds can be dispersed.

Explain how the seeds are being dispersed in each picture.

1. _____

_____

2. _____

_____

3. _____

_____

4. _____

_____

5. _____

_____

6. _____

_____

Parts of a Leaf

Before you can use leaves to help you identify plants, you must know the parts of a leaf. Label the parts of the leaves.

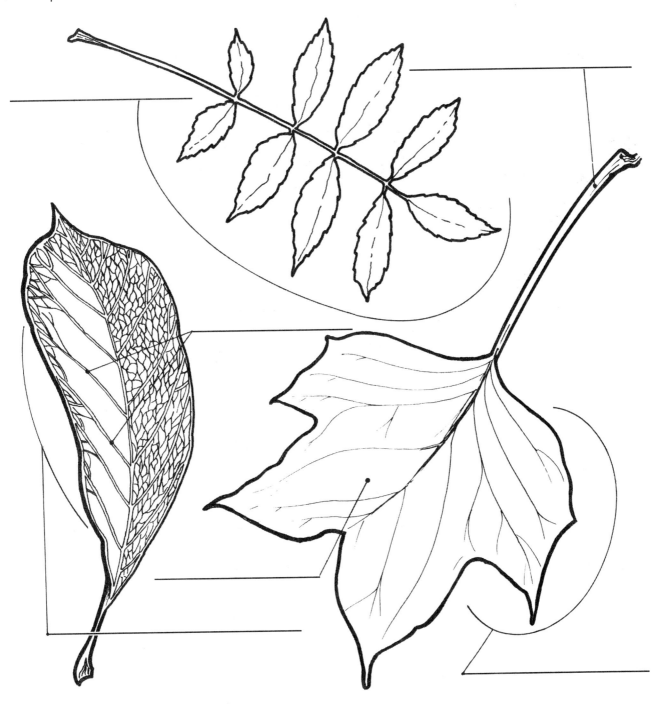

blade	leaflet	lobe
margin	petiole	veins

Leaf Shapes

Label the different characteristics of each group of leaves.

Leaf margin

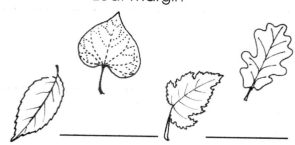

Venation

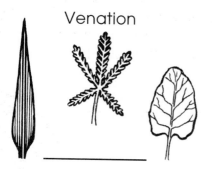

_____ _____

_____ _____ _____ _____

Leaf arrangement
on the stem

Leaf division

_____ _____   _____ _____ _____

Shape of the leaf base

_____ _____ _____ _____ _____

alternate	double saw-toothed	flat
heart	lobed	opposite
palmate	palmate compound	parallel
pinnate	pinnate compound	rounded
saw-toothed	simple	smooth
uneven	v-shaped	

Food Factories

Leaves are the "food factories" for green plants. Structures within a leaf change the energy in sunlight into chemical energy that the plant can use as food.

Label the parts of a leaf.

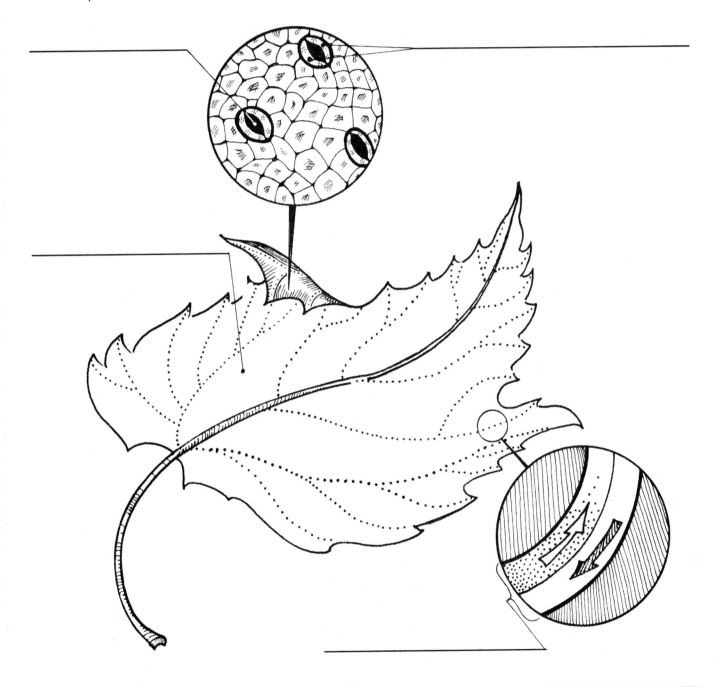

guard cells   stomata   vein   waxy layer

Leaf Cross Section

Label the parts of the cross section of a leaf.

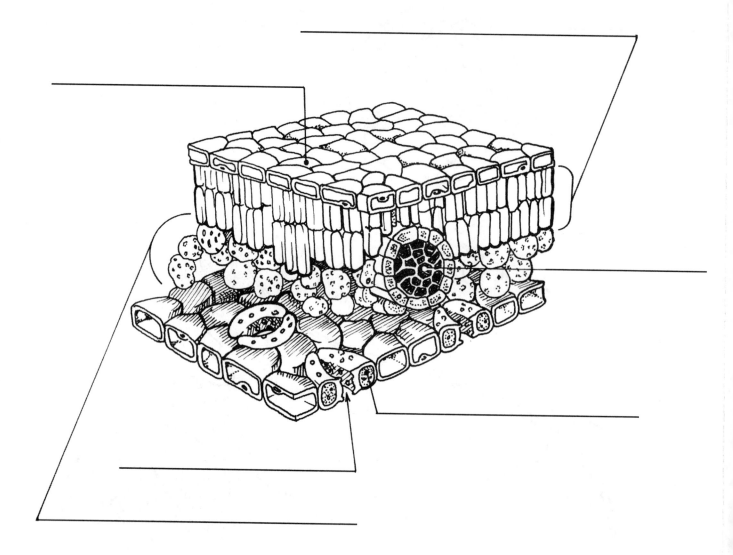

| epidermis | guard cell | palisade layer |
| spongy layer | stoma | vein |

A Key to Trees

A scientist uses a key to identify a tree by its leaves.

Use the following key to identify the leaves pictured.

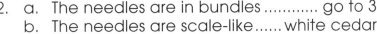

1. a. The tree has needles .... go to 2
    b. The tree has leaves........................ go to 5
2. a. The needles are in bundles .... go to 3
    b. The needles are scale-like...... white cedar
3. a. There are 5 needles .... white pine
    b. There are 2 needles .... go to 4
4. a. The needles are thick and spread
        away from each other .... jack pine
    b. The needles are long and thin..... red pine
5. a. The leaves are simple .... go to 8
    b. The leaves are compound............ go to 6
6. a. The leaflets radiate from
        one point .... go to 7
    b. The leaflets do not radiate from
        one point .... white ash
7. a. There are 5 leaflets .... buckeye
    b. There are 7 leaflets .... horse chestnut
8. a. The leaf has notches..................... go to 9
    b. The leaf does not have notches...go to 10
9. a. The notches are pointed........ silver maple
    b. The notches are rounded...... sugar maple
10. a. The leaf is tapered at
        both ends .... dogwood
    b. The leaf is heart-shaped.............. catalpa

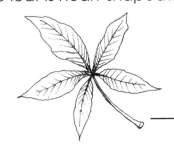

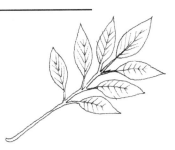

The Tree

Label the three main parts of a tree and the types of tissues in its trunk.

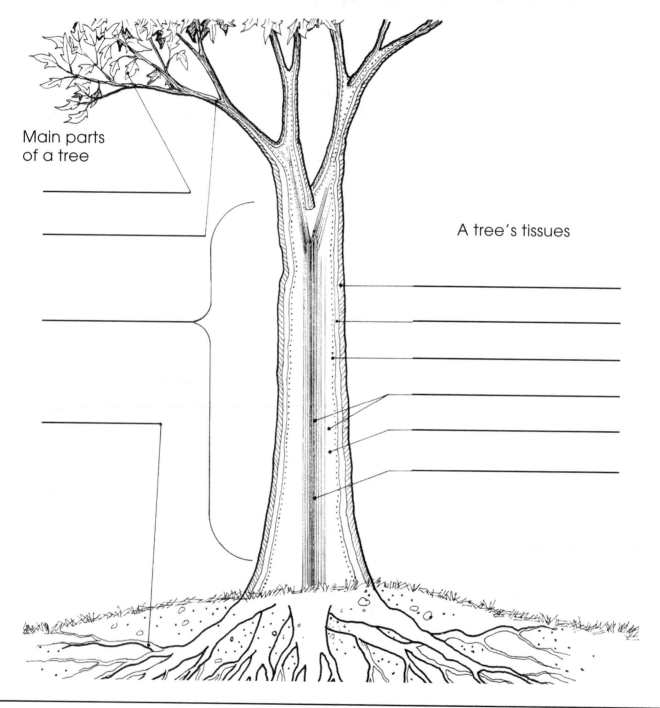

Main parts
of a tree

_____

_____

_____

A tree's tissues

_____

_____

_____

_____

bark	branch	cambium	heartwood
leaf	phloem (inner bark)	root	sapwood
trunk	xylem		

Tree Stems

Label the parts of a tree stem.

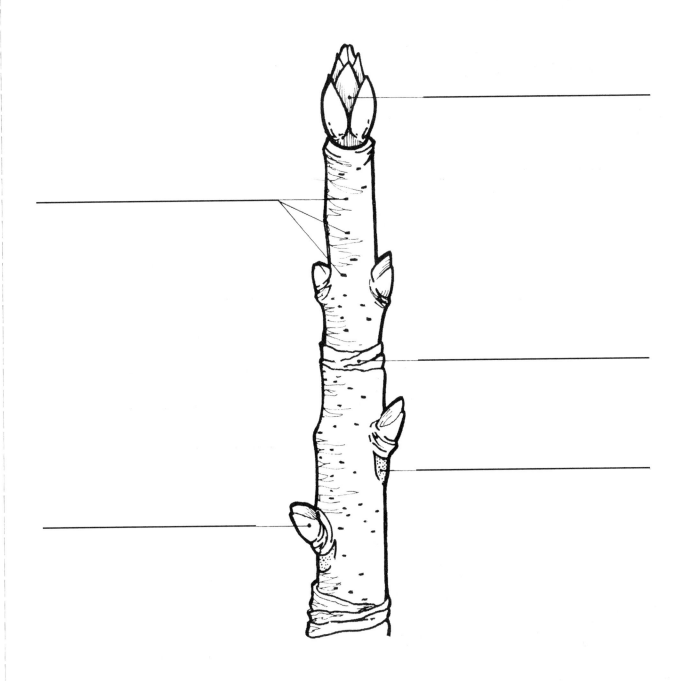

air opening	bud scale scar	end bud
leaf scar	side bud	

Inside a Tree Trunk

Label the parts of the cross section of a tree trunk. Some words may be used more than once.

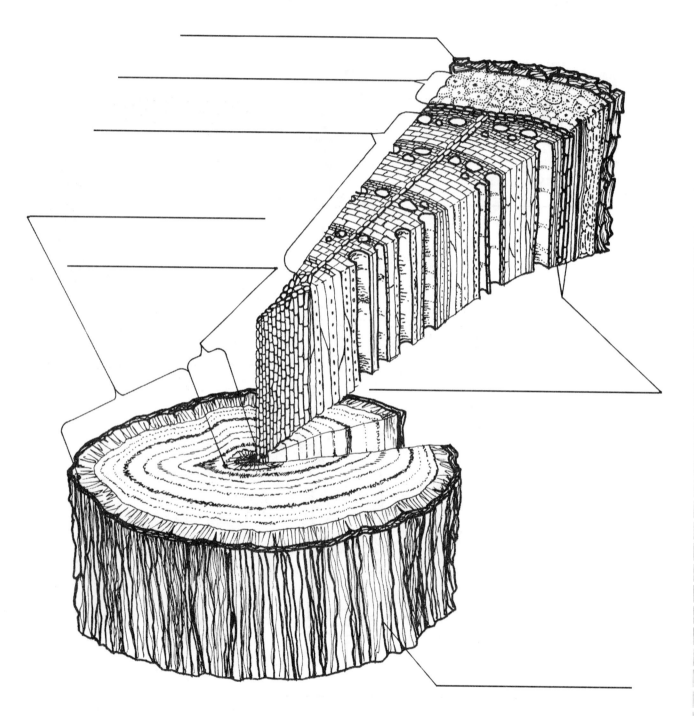

| bark | heartwood | phloem |
| sapwood | vascular cambium | xylem |

Tree History

A freshly cut tree stump can be read like a history book. Label the parts of a tree. Then, study the annual rings, scars, and cuts. Tell what you think happened to the tree.

Tree story:

_____

_____

_____

_____

_____

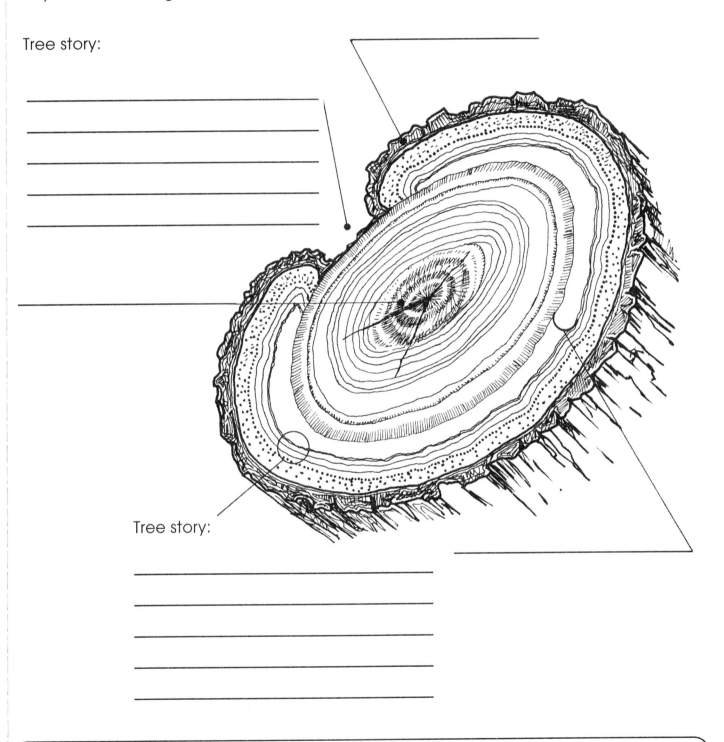

Tree story:

_____

_____

_____

_____

_____

annual ring	bark	heartwood

Underground Stems

Tubers, **rhizomes**, and **bulbs** are three types of underground stems.

Label each type of bulb and its parts. Some words may be used more than once.

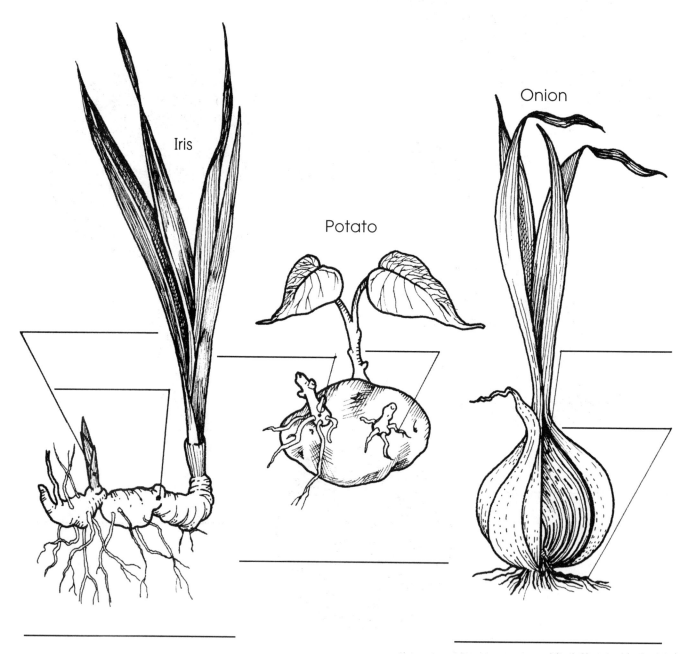

Iris

Potato

Onion

bud	bulb	leaf
rhizome	root	stem
tuber		

Root Systems

Label each root system.

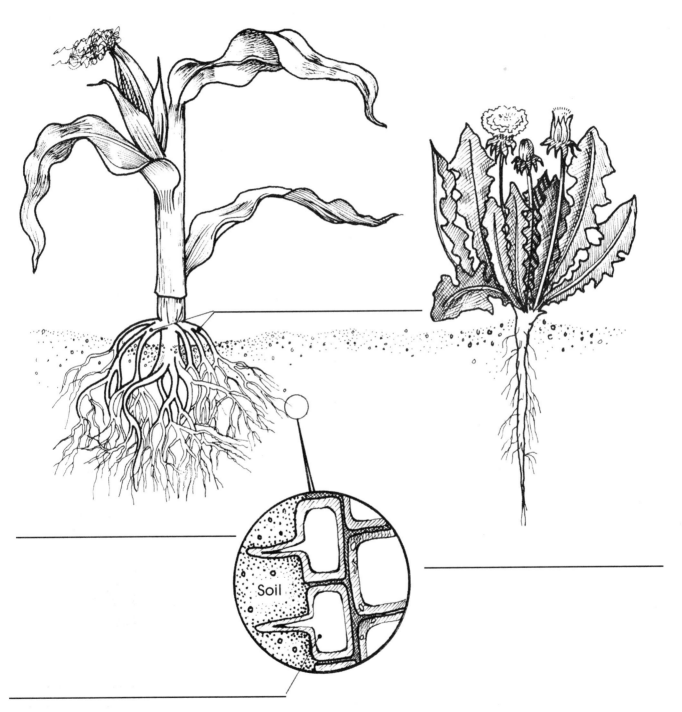

Soil

fibrous root system	prop roots
root hair cell	taproot system

Name

Inside a Root

The diagrams show two views of a root. Label both the top cross-sectional and side cross-sectional views.

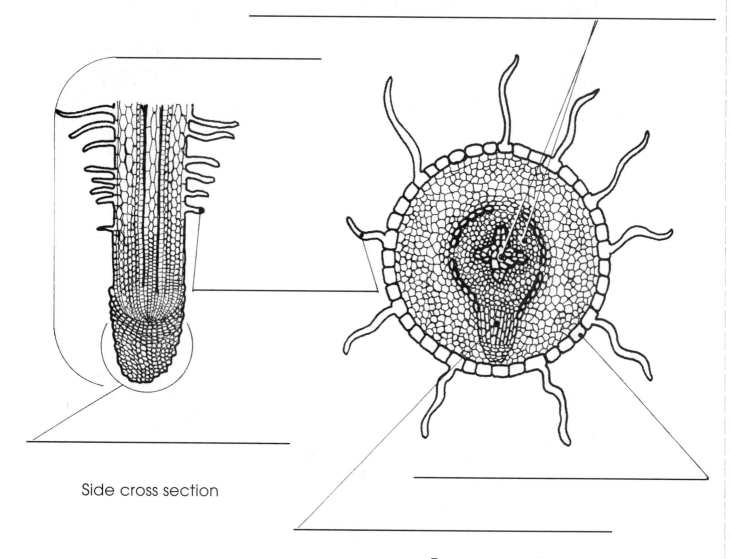

Side cross section

Top cross section
of a young root

branch root	food and water transport system	root cap
root hairs	root tip	surface layer

Life Cycle of a Conifer

Label the active parts in the life cycle of a conifer tree.

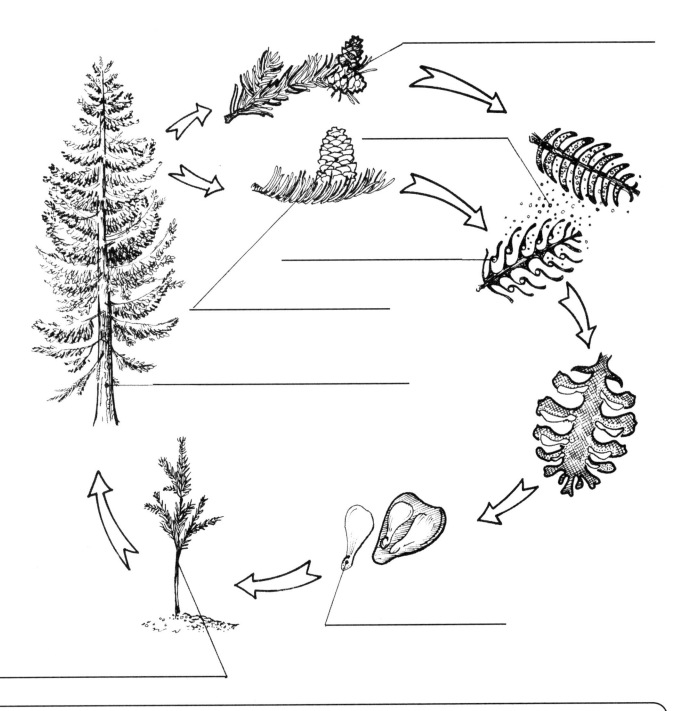

female cone	male cone	mature conifer tree
ovule	pollen	seed
seedling		

Ferns

Label the parts of a fern.

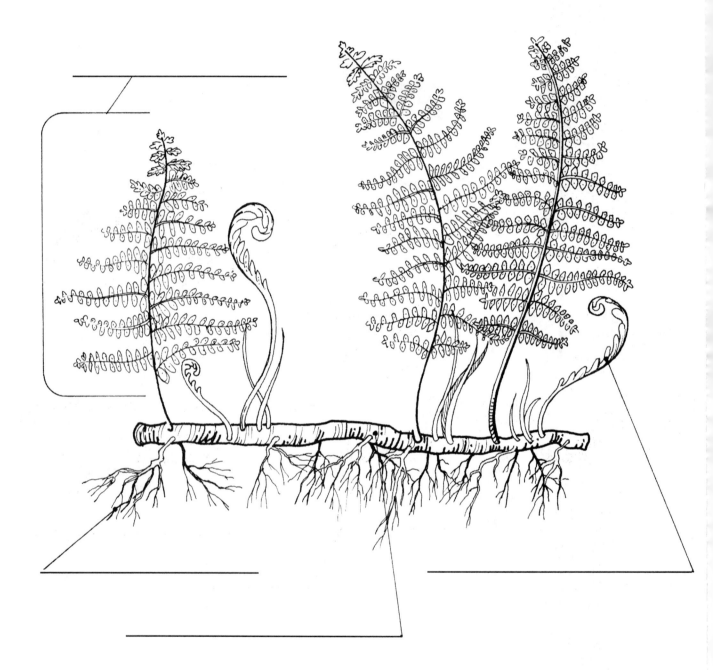

fiddlehead	frond	rhizome
root		

Growth of a Mushroom

Label the parts of a mushroom.

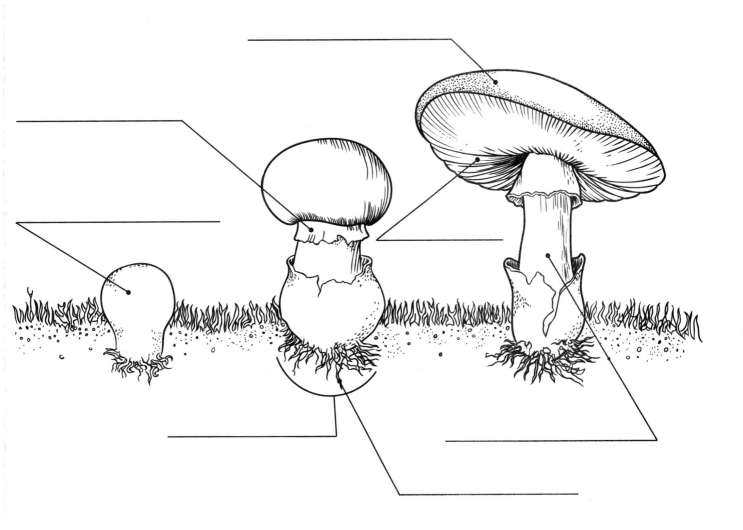

cap	filament	gills	membrane
mycelium	ring (annulus)	stalk	

Animal Kingdom

The animal kingdom is often divided into subgroups called **phyla**.

Draw a line from each animal to the phylum it belongs in. The, draw a line from each animal to its characteristics.

Phylum	Animal	Characteristics

Flatworms

The bodies of these long animals are divided into segments.

Segmented worms

The bodies of these marine animals have slimy plates with spines.

Arthropods

These animals have three body parts and jointed legs.

Mollusks

These animals have a notochord that supports the body.

Echinoderms

These animals have soft, thin, flat bodies.

Chordates

These soft-bodied animals are usually covered by a slimy shell.

Coelenterates

These jelly-like animals usually live in the sea and have cylinder, bell, or umbrella shapes.

Circulatory Systems

The **circulatory system** carries material to every part of the body. It then picks up waste to be removed from the body. Circulatory systems are necessary for continued life in an organism.

Label the parts of the circulatory system for each animal.

two-chambered heart

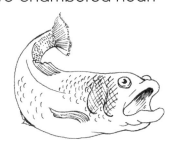 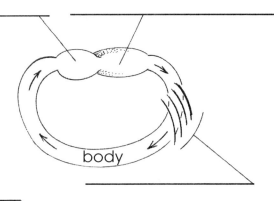

body

three-chambered heart

 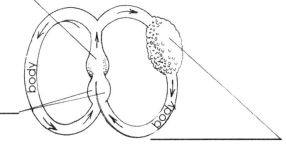

body

body

four-chambered heart

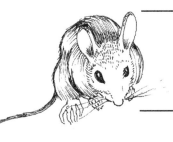 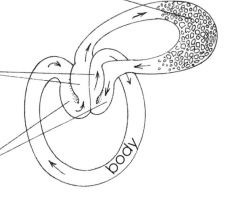

body

Fish	**Lizard**	**Mouse**
atrium	2 atriums	2 atriums
gills	lungs	2 ventricles
ventricle	ventricle	lungs

Animal Defenses

Each of the animals shown has a special defensive adaptation. Name the animal (a).
Then, describe its defensive adaptation (b).

a. _____   a. _____   a. _____
b. _____   b. _____   b. _____
_____   _____   _____

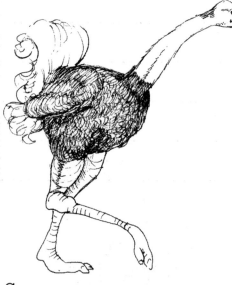 

a. _____   a. _____   a. _____
b. _____   b. _____   b. _____
_____   _____   _____

| opossum | ostrich | porcupine |
| skunk | turtle | walking stick |

Locomotion

Animals have adaptations that allow them to move from place to place in special ways.

Complete the chart by writing a one-word description of each animal's primary method of moving (locomotion). Then, name the body parts involved in this movement.

	Method of locomotion	Body parts that allow this kind of movement
rabbit		
fish		
mole		
blue bird		
spider monkey		
tree frog		

Symmetrical Critters

There are three types of symmetry: **radial**, **bilateral**, and **asymmetrical**.

After reading the descriptions below, label the type of symmetry each animal has.

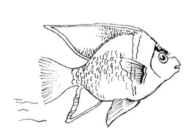

Animal	Kind of symmetry
snail	
starfish	
jellyfish	
angelfish	
sea anemone	
frog	
sponge	
spider	
butterfly	
lobster	

Types of Symmetry

asymmetrical: These animals do not have a definite shape and therefore, no symmetry.

bilateral: The left and right sides are alike and equally proportional.

radial: The body parts are symmetrical around a central point.

Classifying Vertebrates

Vertebrates are sorted into five main groups called **classes**.

Write the name of the class for each vertebrate.

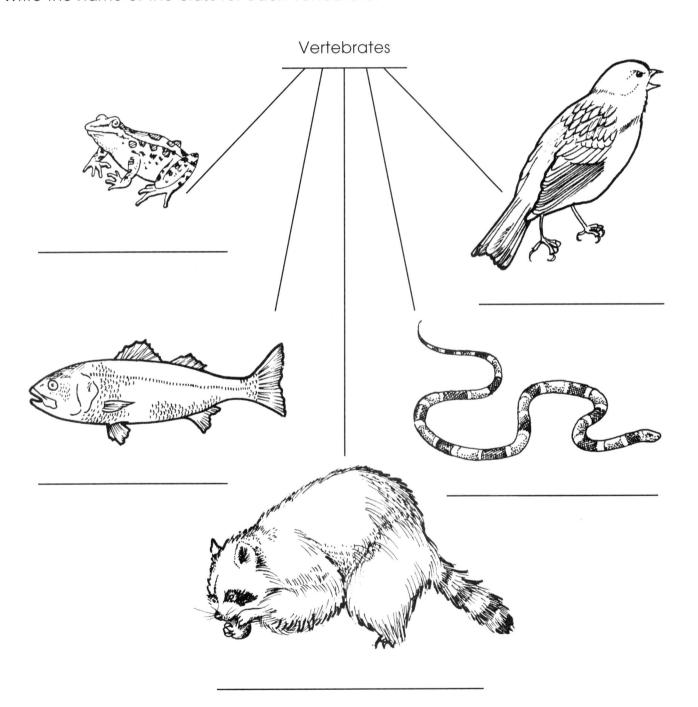

Vertebrates

_____

_____

_____

_____

_____

amphibians   birds   fish   mammals   reptiles

What's a Vertebrate?

Vertebrates are grouped into five different **classes** based on several characteristics. Some classes share characteristics, but they also differ in a few significant ways.

Complete the chart.

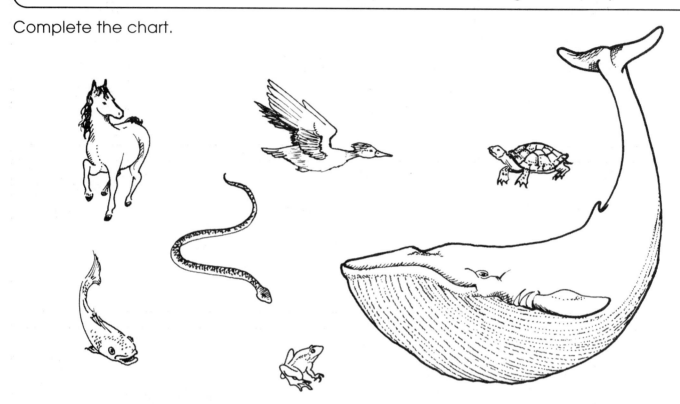

	Fish	Amphibians	Birds	Reptiles	Mammals
body covering					
warm- or cold-blooded					
habitat					
born alive or hatched					
lungs or gills					
chambers in heart					

Classy Vertebrates

Name the class for each vertebrate. Some words will be used more than once.

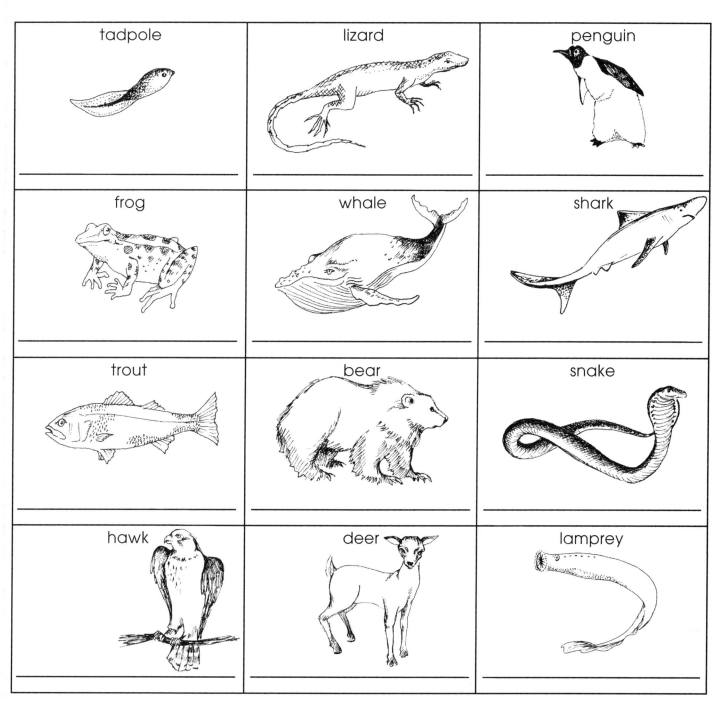

tadpole	lizard	penguin
frog	whale	shark
trout	bear	snake
hawk	deer	lamprey

amphibians   birds   bony fish   cartilaginous fish

jawless fish   mammals   reptiles

Animals with Backbones

Vertebrates are animals that have backbones. They are members of a group called **chordates**.

Write the name of the class for each set of characteristics and give an example of each.

Class	Characteristics	Example
	—skeleton of cartilage —paired fins —cold-blooded —toothlike scales on skin	
	—jawless —sucker-shaped mouth —cartilaginous skeleton —cold-blooded	
	—skeleton of bone —gill covers —scales —cold-blooded	
	—most young have gills —most adults have lungs —lay eggs in water or moist ground —cold-blooded	
	—dry, scaly skin —egg has tough shell —cold-blooded —well-developed lungs	
	—feathers —wings —hollow bones —warm-blooded	
	—have hair at same point in life —feed milk to young —well-developed brain —warm-blooded	

amphibians	bear	birds	bony fish	cartilaginous fish
frog	hawk	jawless fish	lamprey	lizard
mammals	reptiles	shark	trout	

Backbones

Animals with backbones are called **vertebrates**.

Each of these vertebrates belongs to a different class. Color the backbone in each skeleton. Then, name the class of each animal.

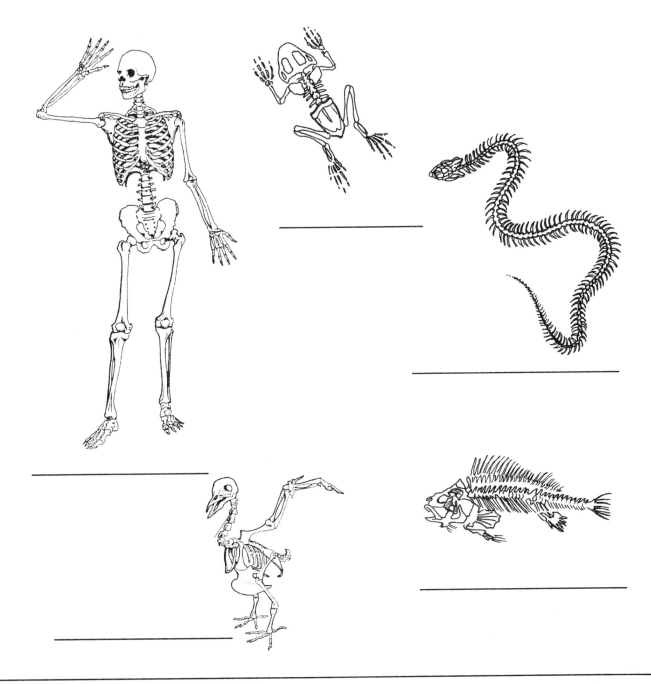

_____

_____

_____

_____

| amphibians | birds | fish | mammals | reptiles |

Vertebrates

Vertebrates, animals with backbones, can be grouped into several classes.

List four characteristics for each class.

Jawless fish

1. _____
2. _____
3. _____
4. _____

Cartilaginous fish

1. _____
2. _____
3. _____
4. _____

Bony fish

1. _____
2. _____
3. _____
4. _____

Amphibians

1. _____
2. _____
3. _____
4. _____

Reptiles

1. _____
2. _____
3. _____
4. _____

Birds

1. _____
2. _____
3. _____
4. _____

Mammals

1. _____
2. _____
3. _____
4. _____

Backbone or No Backbone?

Animals with backbones are called **vertebrates**. Those without backbones are called **invertebrates**.

Label each animal as a *vertebrate* or an *invertebrate*. Then, name each animal.

_____

_____

_____

_____

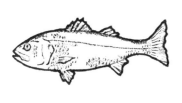

_____

_____

bird	clam	cow	crayfish	dog
fish	fly	horse	starfish	worm

Rippers, Nippers, and Grinders

Most mammals have two or more types of teeth: **incisors** for nipping food like scissors, **canines** for tearing food, and **molars** for grinding food.

Label the teeth on the animals. Some words will be used more than once.

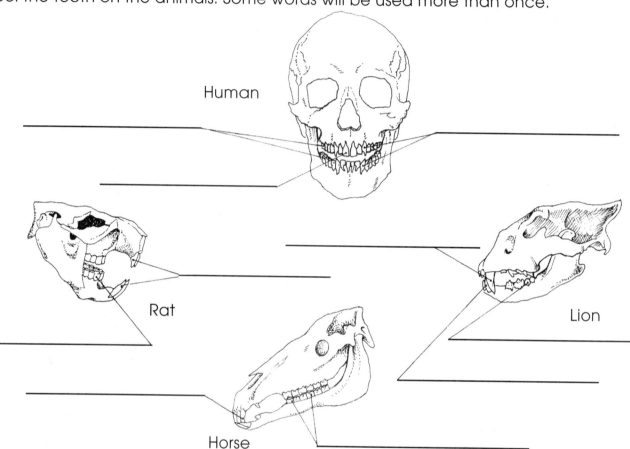

Human

Rat

Lion

Horse

Animal	Type of teeth	Kinds of food eaten
rat		
lion		
horse		
human		

canines　　　dairy products　　　fruits
grains　　　grasses　　　incisors
meats　　　molars　　　vegetables

The Mammal with Wings

Unlike other mammals, bats have true wings. A bat's wings also function like arms.

Label the parts of a bat.

fifth finger	foot	forearm
fourth finger	second finger	tail
third finger	thumb	upper arm
wing membrane		

The Fish—External

Label the external parts of a fish.

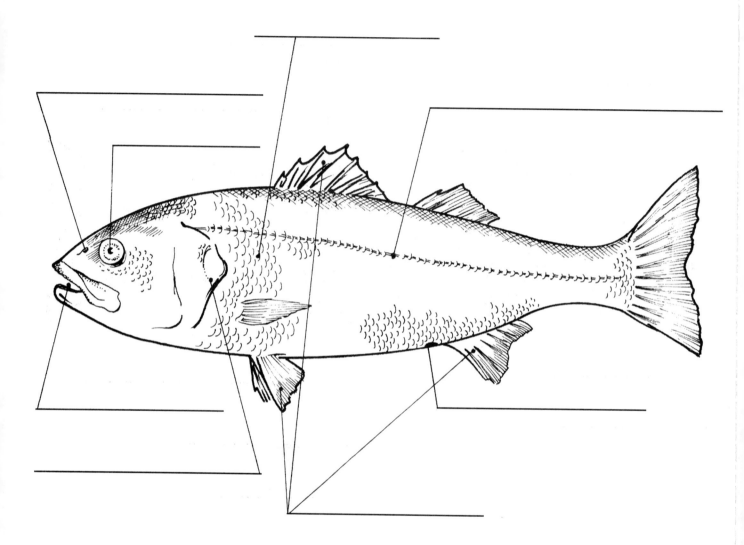

anus	eye	fins	gill cover
lateral line	mouth	nostril	scale

The Fish—Internal

Label the internal parts of a fish.

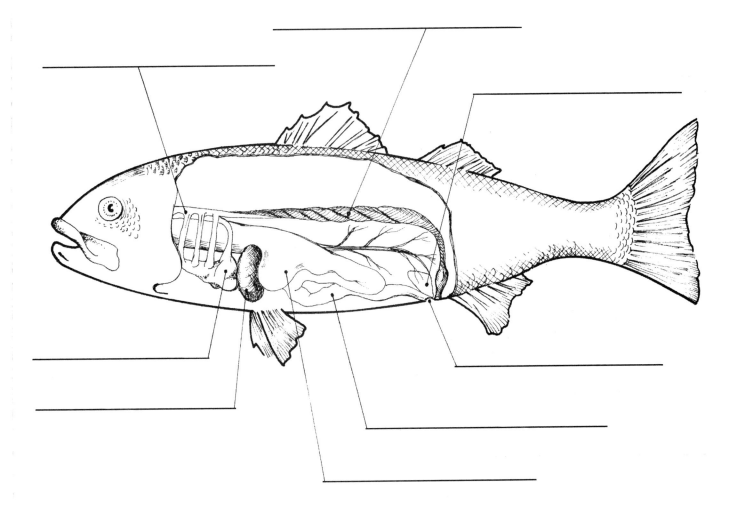

anus	dorsal aorta	heart
intestine	kidney	liver
ovary	stomach	

The Frog—External

Label the external parts of a frog and the parts of the frog's mouth. Some words may be used more than once.

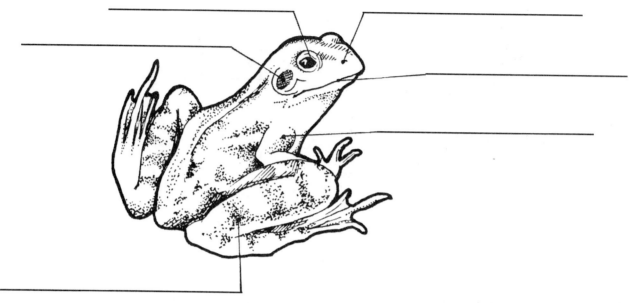

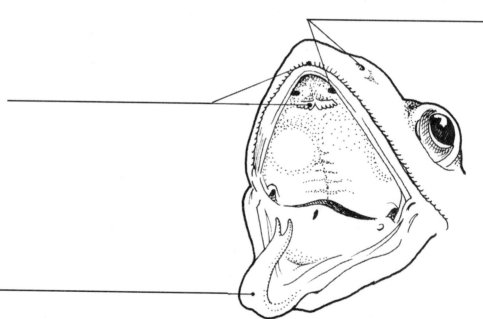

eardrum	eye	foreleg
hind leg	mouth	nostril
teeth	tongue	

The Frog—Internal

Label the internal parts of a frog.

anus	heart	kidney
large intestine	liver	lung
mesentery	small intestine	stomach

Life Cycle of a Frog

Label the steps in the life cycle of a frog.

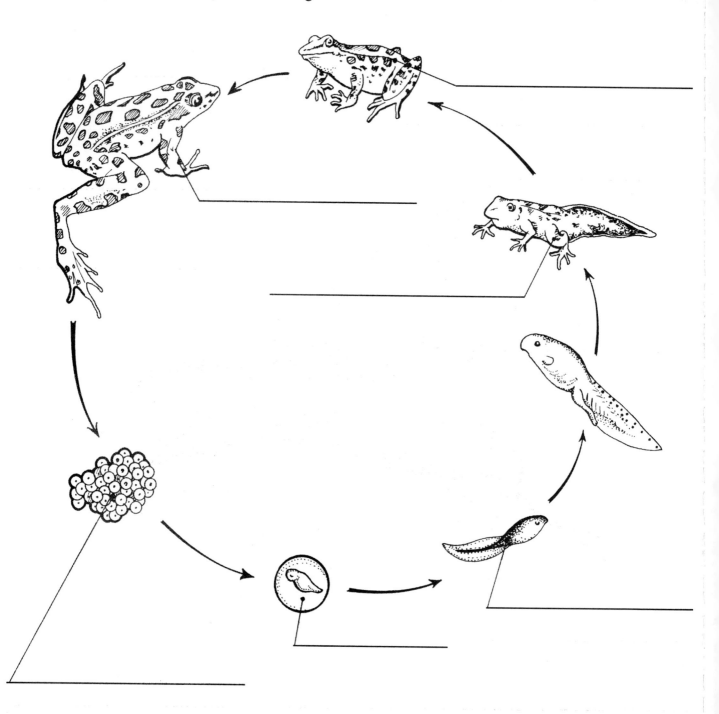

adult frog	egg	egg mass
froglet	tadpole	young frog

Pit Viper

Label the parts of the head of a pit viper.

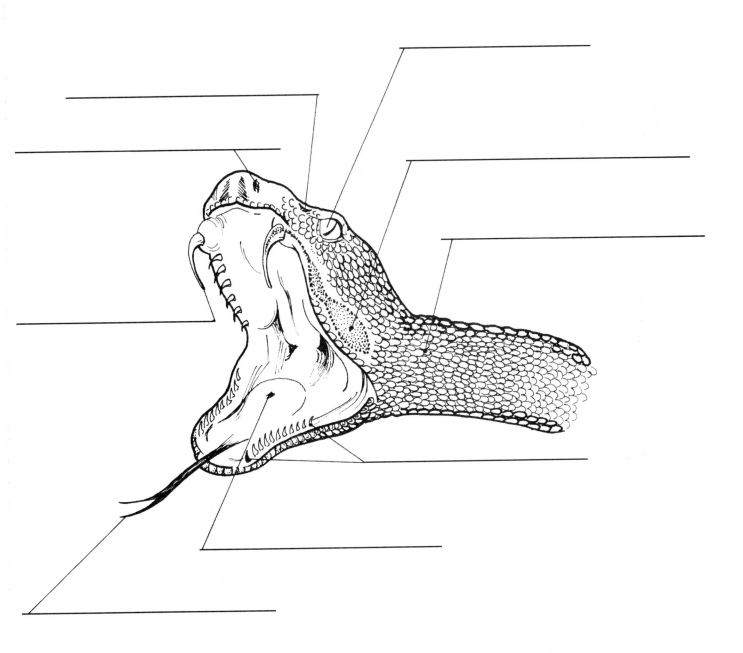

eye	fang	glottis (windpipe)
nostril	pit	scaly skin
teeth	tongue	venom sac

The Bird

Label the parts of a bird.

back	beak	belly
breast	crown	primaries
secondaries	tail feathers	throat

Name_____

Feathers and Wings

The wings and body of a bird are covered with different types of feathers.

Parts of a Wing

Label the three groups of feathers on the wing.

Feathers

Label the three types of feathers.

_____   _____   _____

body feather	coverts
down feather	primary flight feather
primary flight feathers	secondary flight feathers

Bird Bones

Label the major bone structures of a bird.

beak	breastbone	feet
leg bones	pelvic girdle	rib
skull	vertebrae	wing bones

Feathered Friends' Feet

A bird's feet can tell you many things about its habits or home.

Tell how each bird uses its feet.

_____

_____

_____

_____

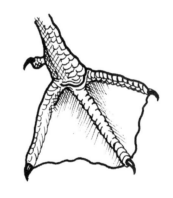

_____

_____

_____

_____

for catching prey
for grasping while climbing
for perching on branches
for swimming
for wading in mud

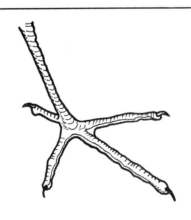

_____

_____

Bird Beaks

The shape of a bird's beak will often tell you what the bird eats.

Tell how each bird uses its beak to eat food.

_____

_____

_____

_____

_____

_____

_____

_____

_____

_____

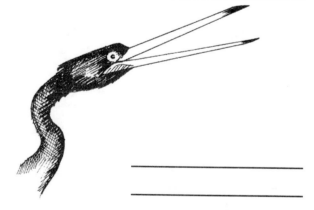

_____

_____

for pounding holes to find insects

to scoop large mouthfuls of water and fish

to suck nectar from flowers

to crack open seeds

to stab small fish

to tear the flesh of animals

More Bird Beaks

The shape of a bird's beak will often tell what kind of food the bird eats.

Describe the feeding habits of each bird.

_____

_____

_____

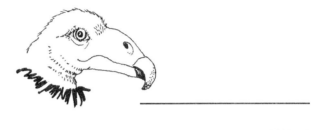

_____

_____

_____

_____

_____

_____

_____

_____

_____

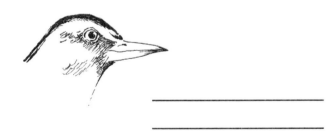

_____

_____

_____

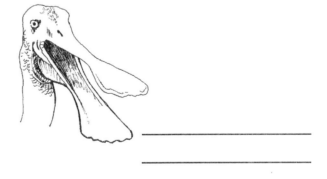

_____

_____

_____

cracks nuts and seeds

scoops fish from water

tears flesh

grabs and holds worms

sweeps back and forth through water to filter out tiny plants and animals

traps insects in midair

Strangers in the Night

It is much easier to identify a bird when you can see its coloring, size, and shape. At night, this is usually difficult.

Identify each bird by its silhouette.

barn swallow	blue jay	cardinal
great blue heron	horned owl	hummingbird
kingfisher	pelican	pheasant
robin		

Highways for the Birds

A **flyway** is the path that migrating birds will follow, often traveling great distances.

Label each of the major flyways found in North America.

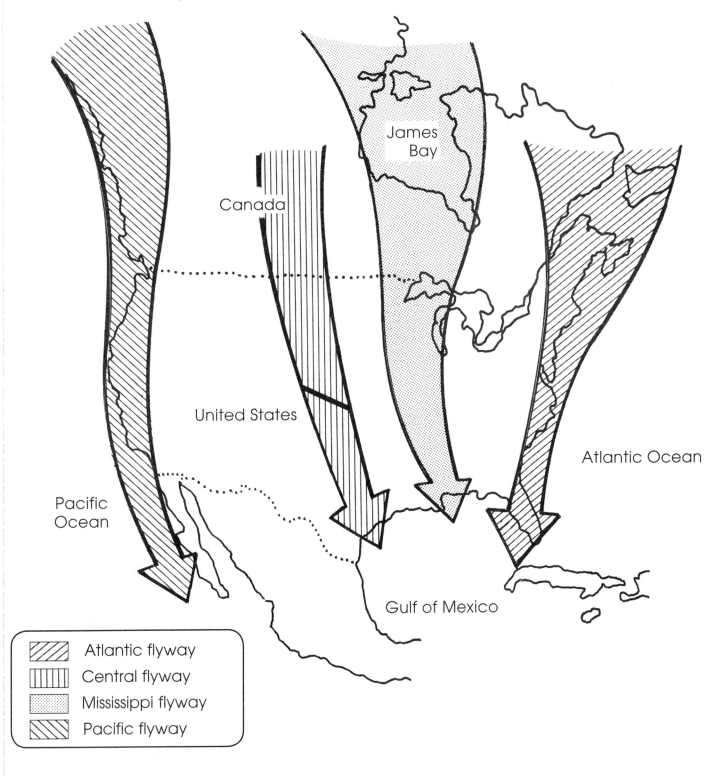

James Bay

Canada

United States

Pacific Ocean

Atlantic Ocean

Gulf of Mexico

Atlantic flyway
Central flyway
Mississippi flyway
Pacific flyway

Bird Eggs

Label the parts of an egg.

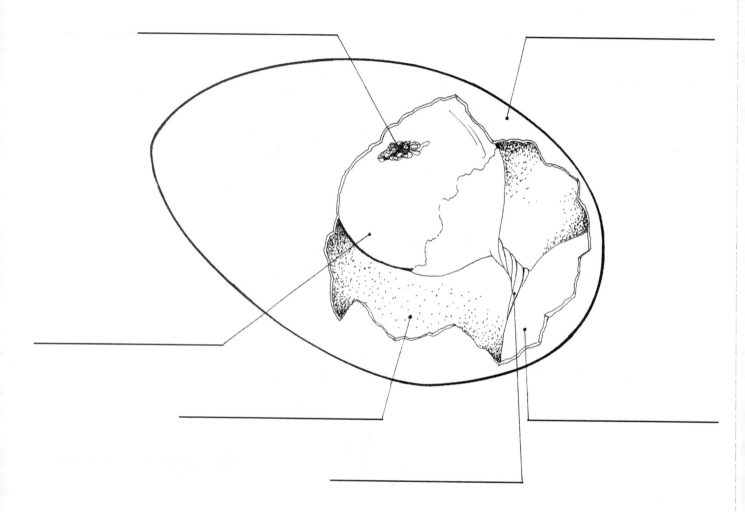

| air space | albumen | chalaza |
| germ | shell | yolk |

Chicken Eggs

Label the parts of a fertilized hen's egg.

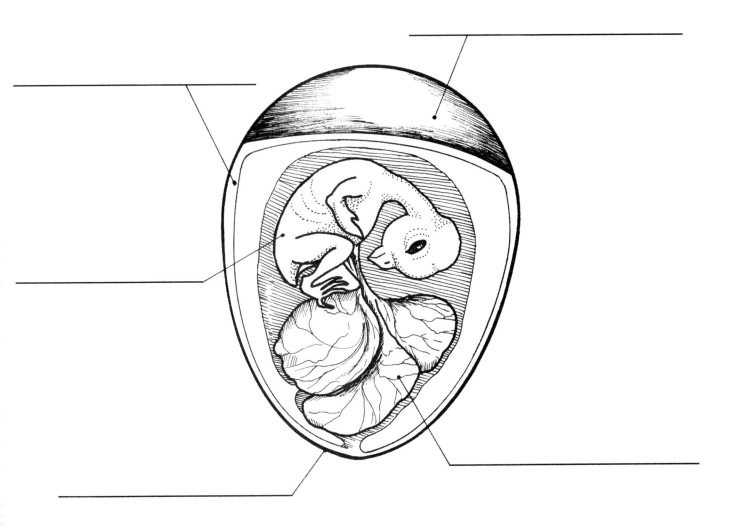

air space   embryo   membrane
shell   yolk

Classes of Arthropods

Arthropods are animals that have jointed legs. Three-fourths of all of the different animal types belong to this group.

Write the name of the class for each set of characteristics and give an example of each.

Class	Characteristics	Example
	—round —segmented body —two pairs of legs per segment	
	—flat —segmented body —one pair of legs per segment	
	—hard —flexible exoskeleton —gills —two pairs of antennae —two body sections	
	—two body sections —no antennae —four pairs of legs	
	—three body sections —one pair of antennae —three pairs of legs	

Arachnida	bee	centipede
Chilopoda	Crustacea	Diplopoda
Insecta	lobster	millipede
spider		

Name_____

The Crayfish

Label the parts of a crayfish.

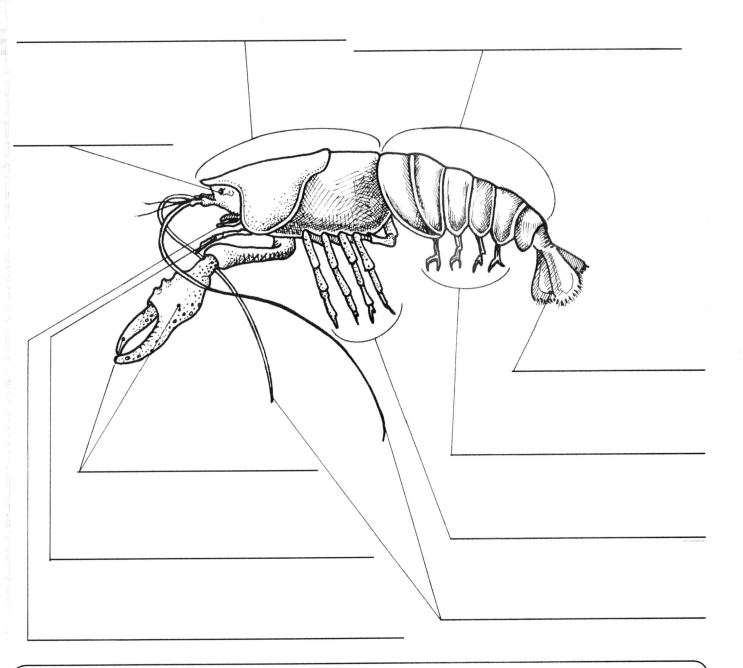

abdomen	antennae	cephalothorax
cheliped	eye	mandible
maxilliped	swimmerets	telson
walking legs		

Insect Orders

The major groups of insects are called **orders**. Below are examples from seven of the most common orders of insects.

Label each insect and its order.

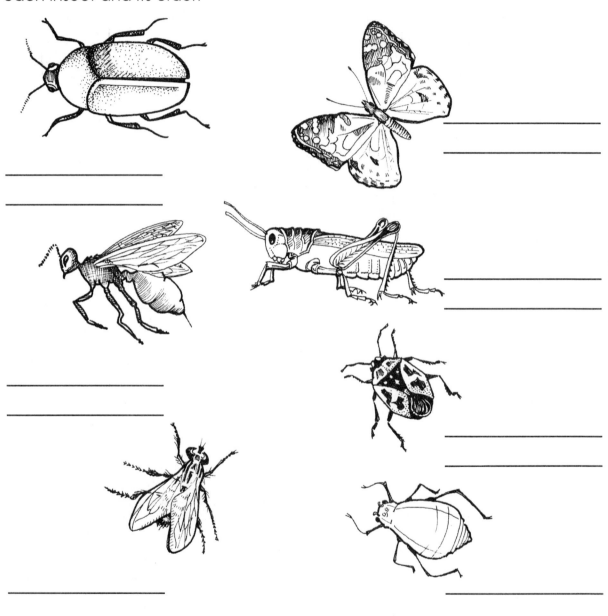

_____

_____

_____

_____

_____

_____

_____

_____

_____

_____

_____

_____

_____

_____

bees and wasps (Hymenoptera)	beetles (Coleoptera)
butterflies and moths (Lepidoptera)	flies (Diptera)
grasshoppers (Orthoptera)	leafhoppers (Homoptera)
true bugs (Hemiptera)	

Orderly Insects

There are more than 25 different orders of insects. Seven of the most common orders are shown.

Write the name of the insects pictured under the correct order.

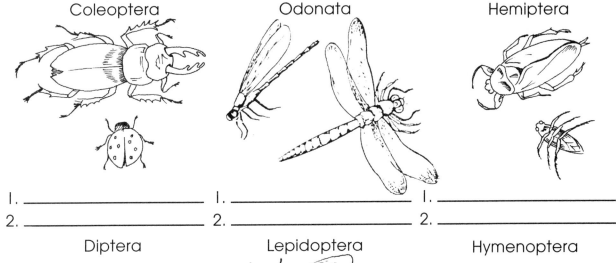

Coleoptera	Odonata	Hemiptera

1. _____   1. _____   1. _____

2. _____   2. _____   2. _____

Diptera	Lepidoptera	Hymenoptera

1. _____   1. _____   1. _____

2. _____   2. _____   2. _____

Orthoptera

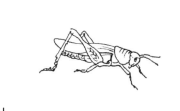 

1. _____   2. _____

ant	backswimmer	butterfly	damselfly
dragonfly	giant water bug	grasshopper	honeybee
housefly	ladybug	mosquito	praying mantis
silkworm moth	stag beetle		

Spiders and Insects

Spiders are not insects. Both spiders and insects are invertebrates. But, spiders are not insects because they have some characteristics that are different from insects, such as having four pairs of legs.

Label the parts of a spider and an insect. Some words may be used more than once.

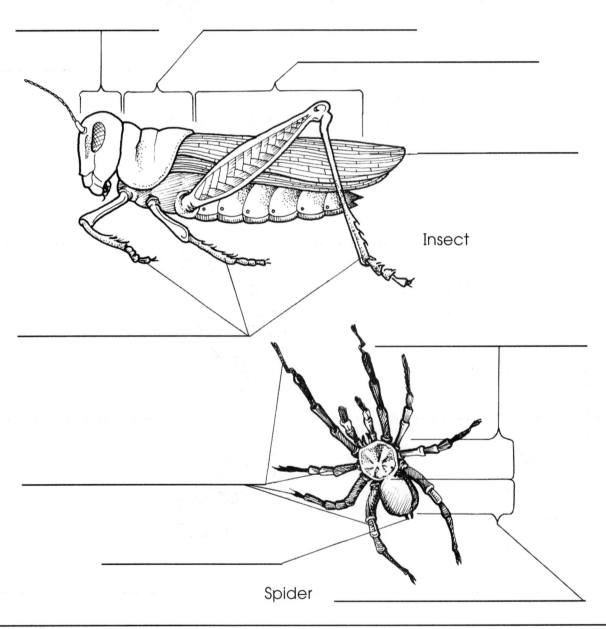

Insect

Spider _____

3 pairs of legs	4 pairs of legs	abdomen
cephalothorax	head	spinneret
thorax	wings	

Common Water Insects

Identify these common water insects.

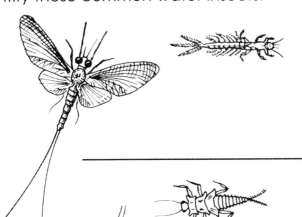 

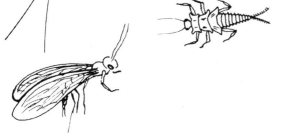 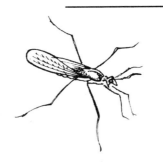

_____   _____

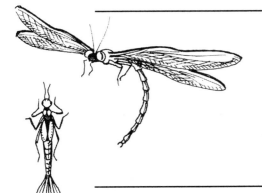 

_____   _____

_____   _____

backswimmer	caddisfly	damselfly
diving beetle	mayfly	stonefly
water strider	whirligig beetle	

The Worker Bee

Label the parts of a worker bee.

abdomen	antenna	antenna cleaner
pollen basket	pollen combs	spur
stinger	thorax	wax scales
wing		

Name_____

The Life Cycle of a Bee

Label the stages of a bee's life cycle.

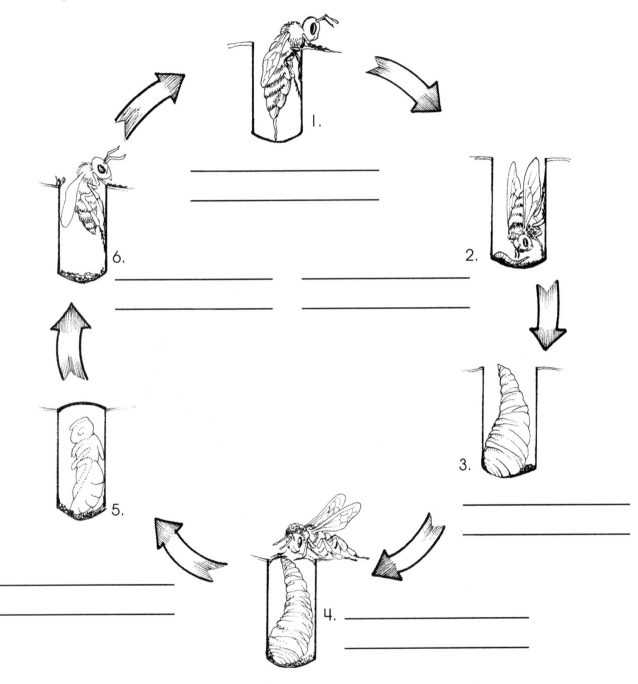

1. _____

_____
_____

6. _____

_____ _____

_____ _____

2. _____

3. _____

_____
_____

5. _____

_____
_____

4. _____

_____

egg laid by queen	full-grown bee grub
grub becomes a pupa	grub fed by worker
grub sealed in its cell	young adult leaves cell

The Ant

Label the parts of an ant's body.

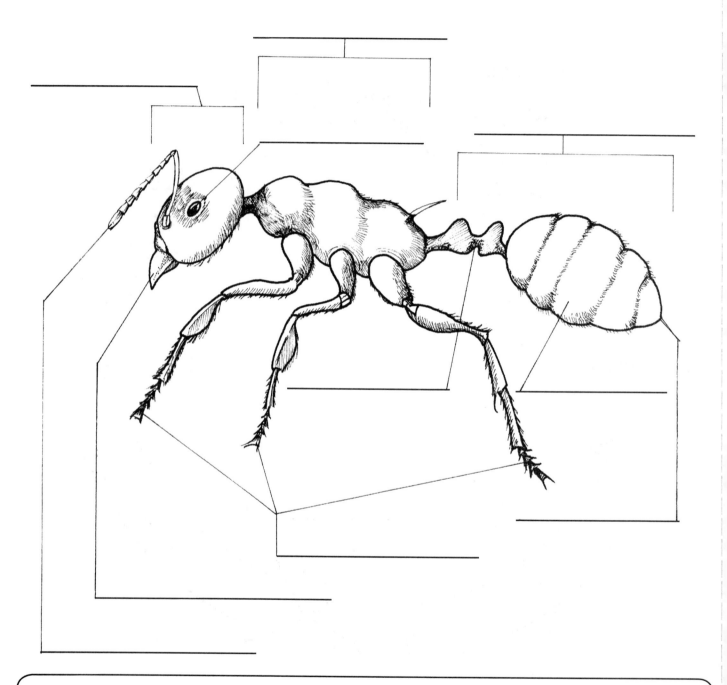

antenna	eye	gaster
head	legs	mandibles
metasoma	sting	trunk
waist		

The Life Cycle of an Ant

Label the stages of an ant's life cycle.

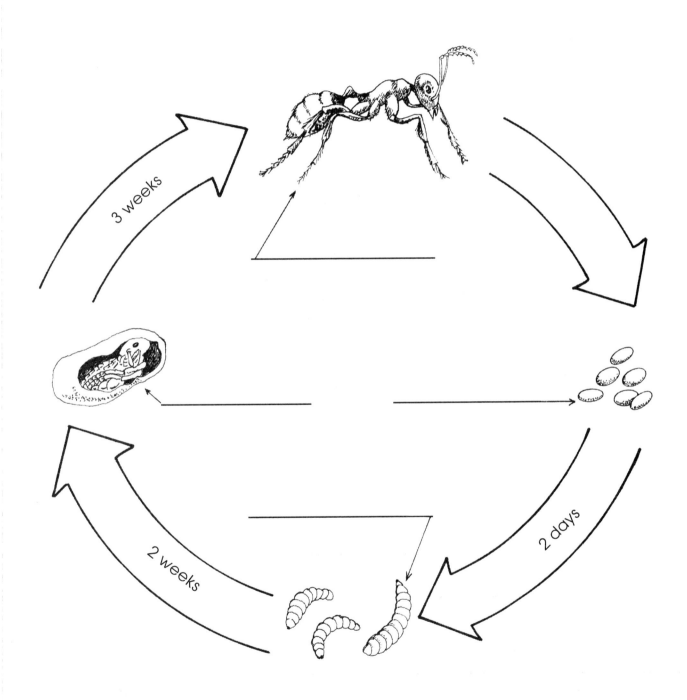

| adult | eggs | larvae | pupa |

The Grasshopper

Label the parts of a grasshopper.

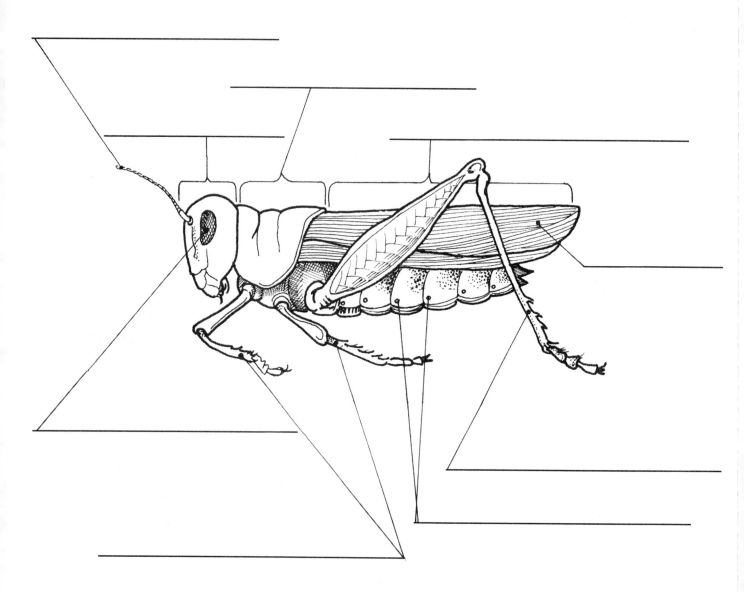

abdomen	antenna	compound eye
head	jumping leg	spiracles
thorax	walking legs	wing

The Grasshopper's Life Cycle

The grasshopper's life cycle is an example of **gradual metamorphosis**. Gradual metamorphosis in insects is where the immature stages are similar in appearance to the adult stage, except smaller and without reproductive capabilities. It is also referred to as **simple metamorphosis**.

Label the stages of a grasshopper's life cycle.

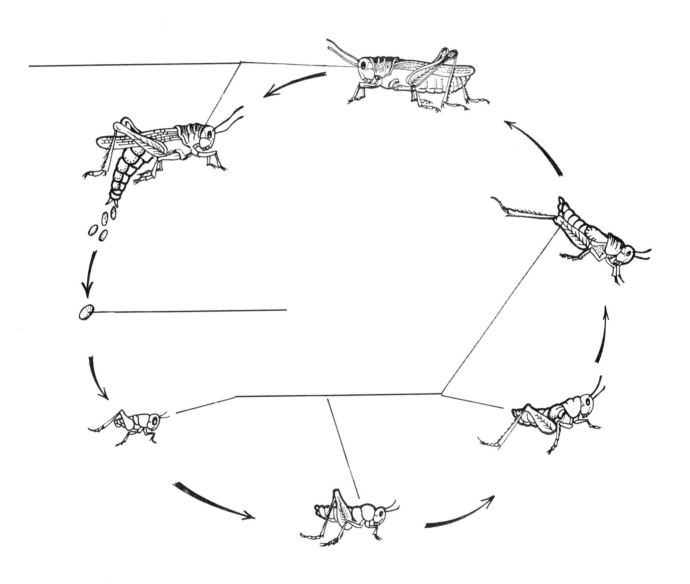

| adult | egg | nymph |

Butterflies and Moths

Butterflies and moths belong to the order of insects called Lepidoptera. Moths and butterflies each have special characteristics to help you tell them apart.

Label the parts of the butterfly. Then, label the special characteristics as either *butterfly* or *moth*.

Moth or Butterfly?

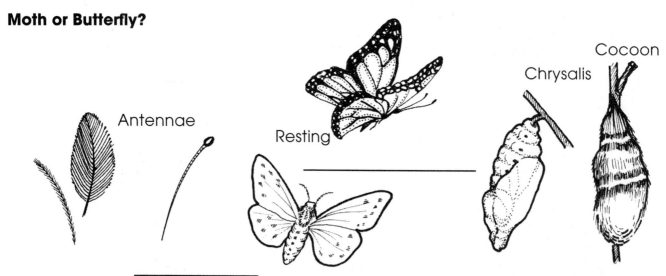

Antennae

Resting

Chrysalis

Cocoon

abdomen	antennae	eye
forewing	head	hind wing
thorax		

The Monarch's Life Cycle

The life cycle of a monarch butterfly is an example of **complete metamorphosis**. Complete metamorphosis is when an insect passes through four separate stages of growth: egg, larva, pupa, and adult. Each stage looks distinct.

Label the stages of a monarch butterfly's life cycle.

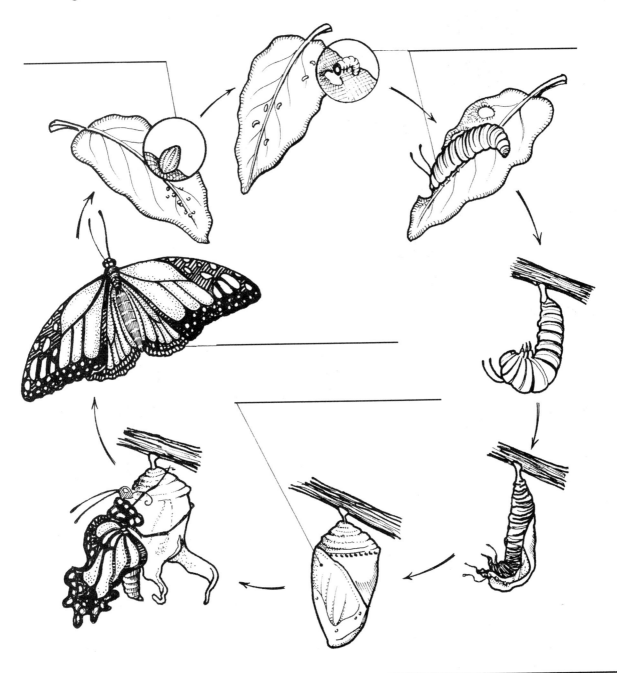

| adult | egg | larva (caterpillar) | pupa in chrysalis |

Metamorphosis

Label the stages of complete and incomplete metamorphosis. Some words may be used more than once.

_____ Metamorphosis

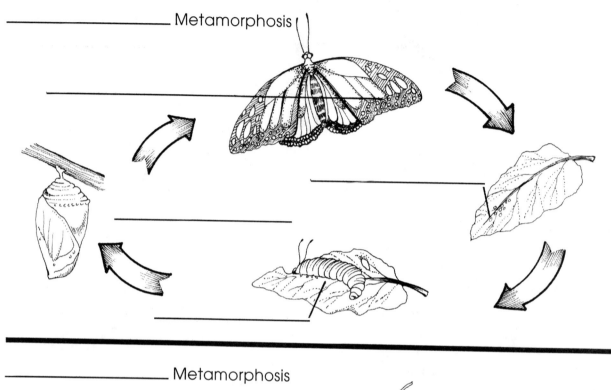

_____ Metamorphosis

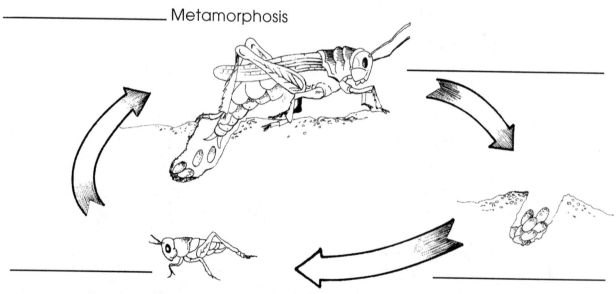

adult	Complete	egg	Incomplete
larva (caterpillar)	nymph	pupa (in chrysalis)	

The Clam

Label the parts of a clam.

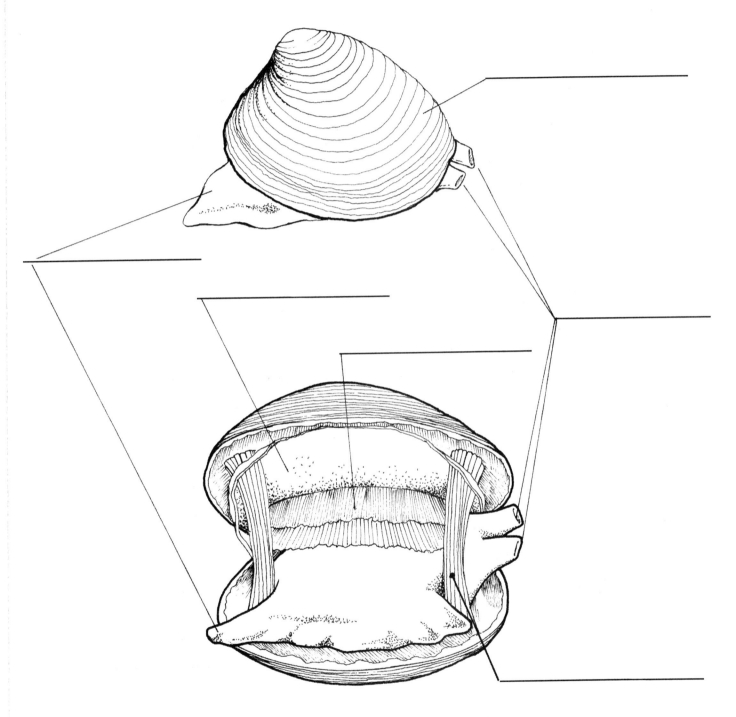

foot	gills	mantle
muscle	shell	siphons

The Starfish

Label the parts of a starfish.

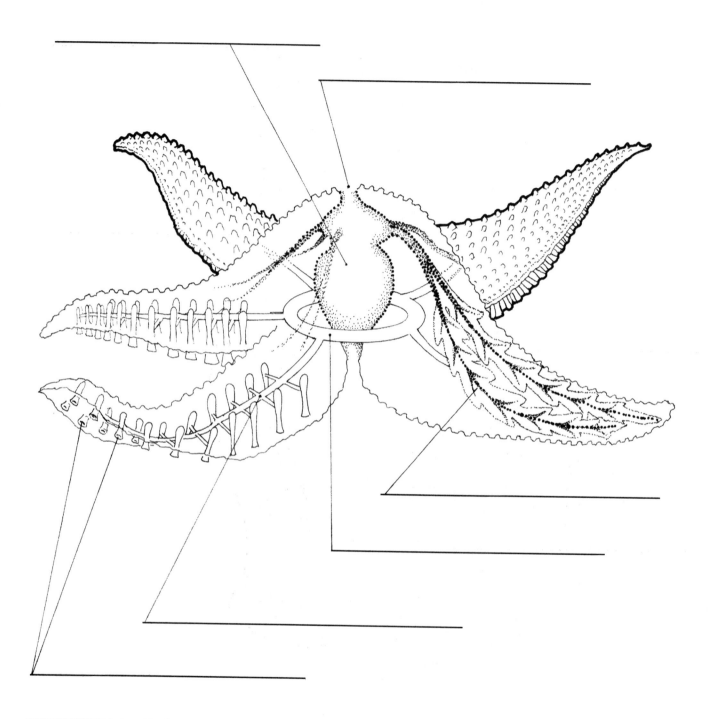

anus	digestive glands	radial canal
ring canal	stomach	tube feet

Name_____

The Sponge

Label the parts of a sponge.

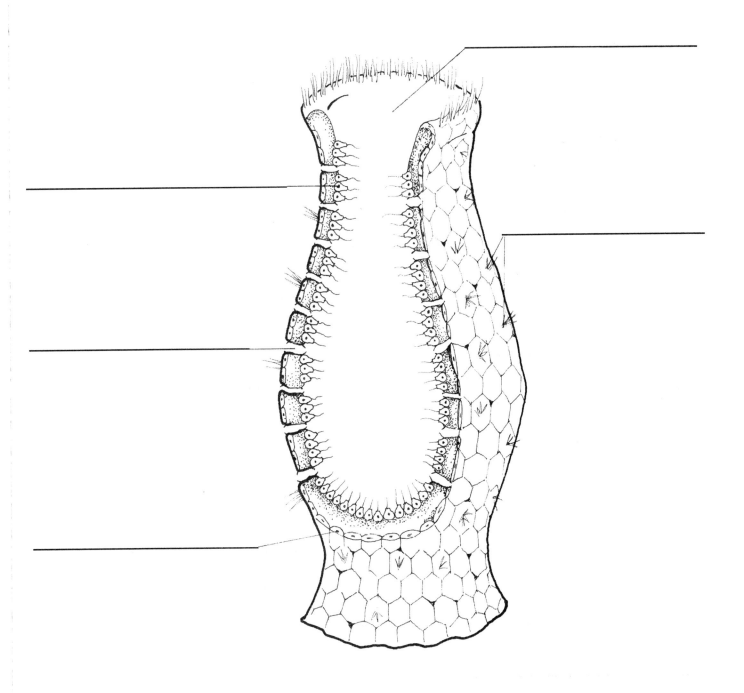

collar cell	epidermal cell	osculum
pore	spicules	

The Hydra

Label the parts of a hydra.

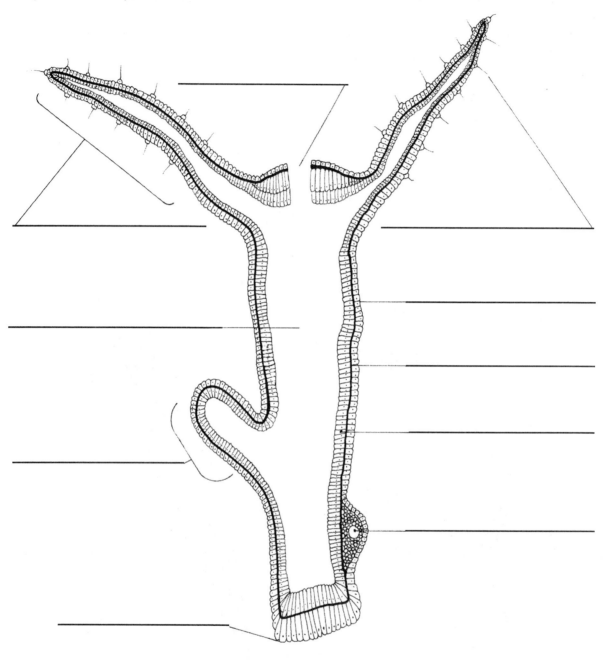

basal disc	bud	ectoderm
endoderm	gastrovascular cavity	mesoglea
mouth	nematocyst	ovary
tentacle		

The Planarian

A **planarian** is a small flatworm that can regenerate missing body parts when portions are cut off.

Label the parts of the regenerated planarian.

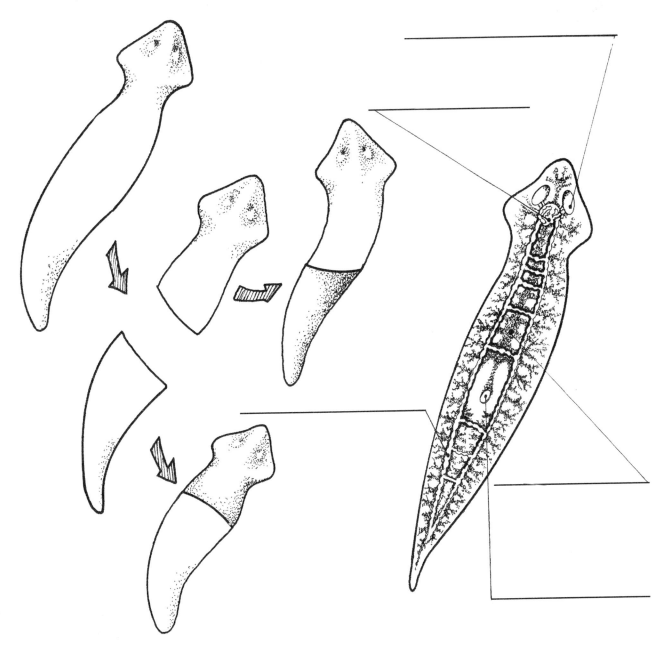

| brain (ganglia) | eyespot | intestine |
| mouth | nerves | |

Worms

There are thousands of different kinds of worms. Each kind belongs to one of the four major groups of worms.

Draw a line from each worm to the group to which it belongs.

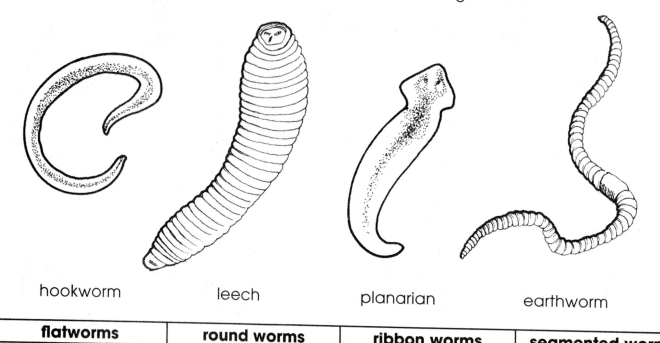

| hookworm | leech | planarian | earthworm |

| **flatworms** | **round worms** | **ribbon worms** | **segmented worms** |

| ascaris | liver fluke | tapeworm | bootlace worm |

More Worms

A **key** is a tool used by scientists to help them identify living things.

Use the key to identify each worm.

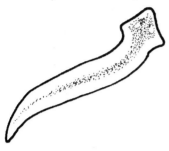

1. Is the body round?
   Yes ....go to 3
   No ....go to 2
2. Is the body short with eyespots?
   Yes .... planarian
   No ....tapeworm
3. Does the body have segments?
   Yes ....go to 4
   No .... ascaris
4. Is the body short?
   Yes ....leech
   No ....go to 5
5. Does the body have a clitellum present?
   Yes .... earthworm
   No ....sandworm

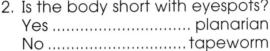

_____

_____

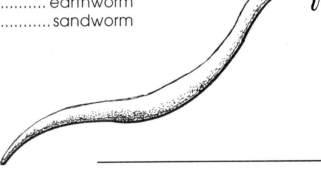

_____

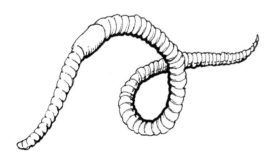

_____

_____

ascaris	earthworm	leech
planarian	sandworm	tapeworm

The Earthworm

Label the external parts of an earthworm.

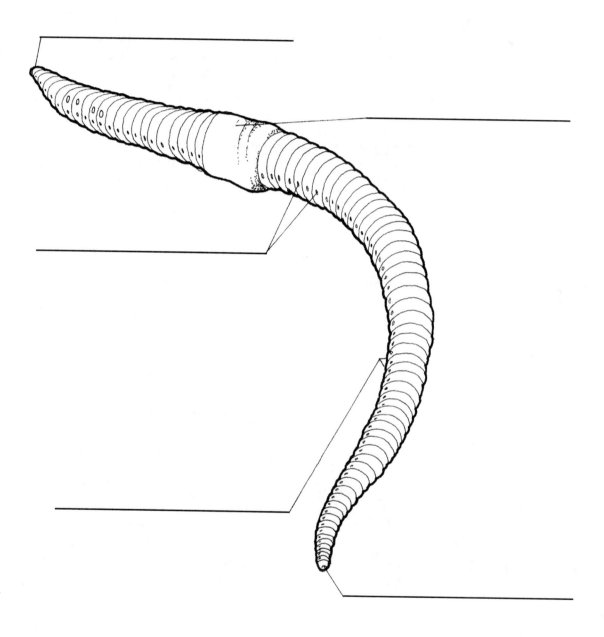

anus   clitellum   mouth

segment   setae

Name_____

The Earthworm's Circulatory System

The earthworm's circulatory system is very simple.

Label the parts of an earthworm and its circulatory system.

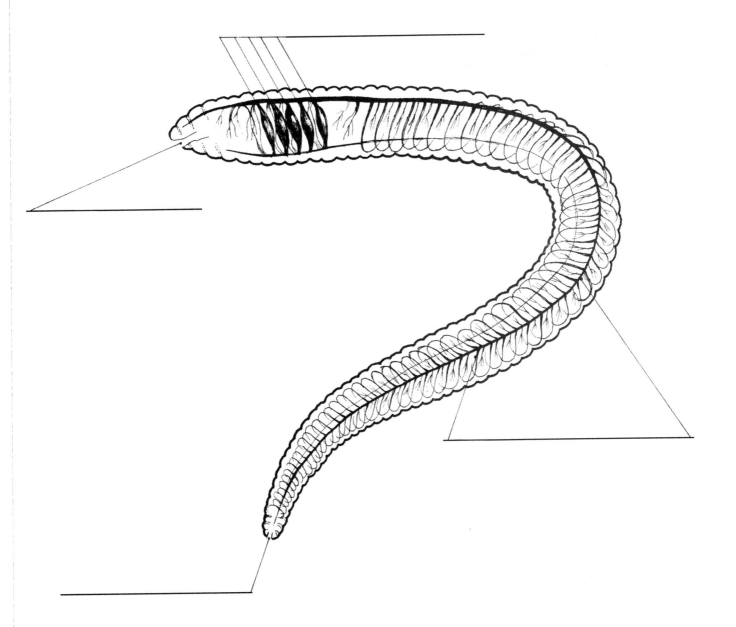

anus	blood vessels	hearts	mouth

The Earthworm's Digestive System

In the earthworm, as in most animals, digestion takes place in a long tube with openings at both ends. This tube is divided into organs that have different jobs.

Label the parts of an earthworm's digestive system.

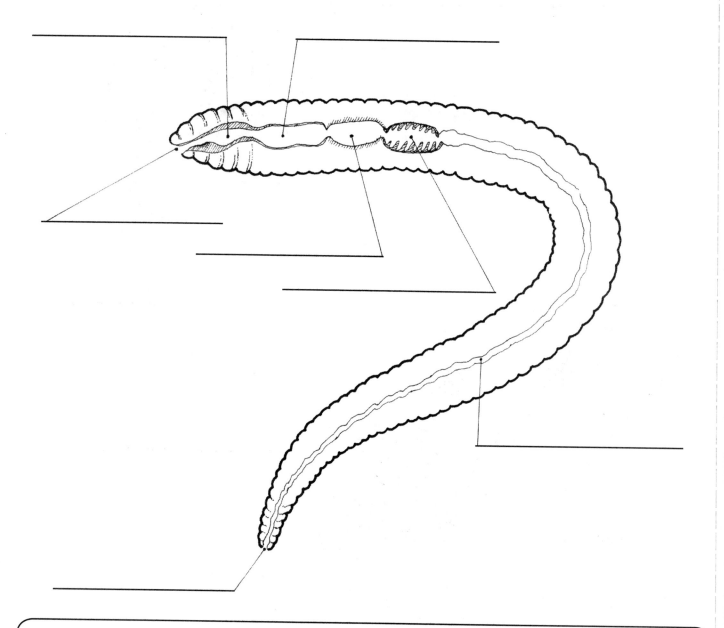

anus	crop	esophagus
gizzard	intestine	mouth
pharynx		

Name_____

Plant and Animal Cells

Plant and animal cells are alike in many ways. But, there are also ways in which they differ. Label the parts of the plant and animal cells. Some words may be used more than once.

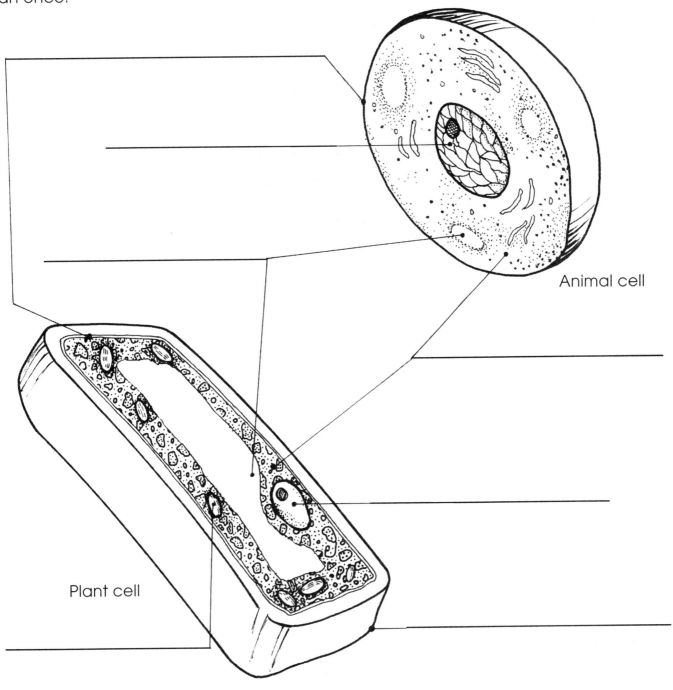

Animal cell

Plant cell

cell membrane	cell wall	chloroplast
cytoplasm	nucleus	vacuole

The Amoeba

Label the parts of a reproducing amoeba.

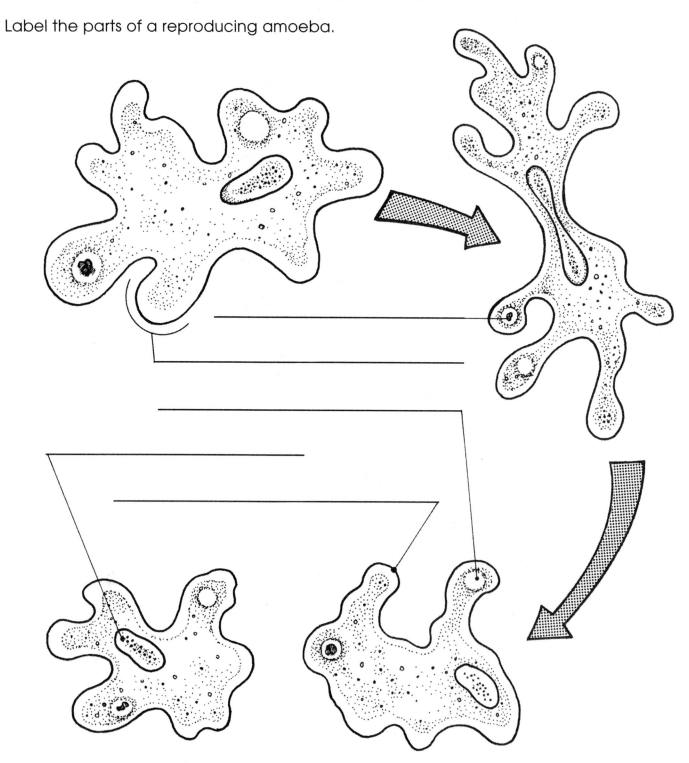

| cell membrane | false foot | food vacuole |
| nucleus | water vacuole | |

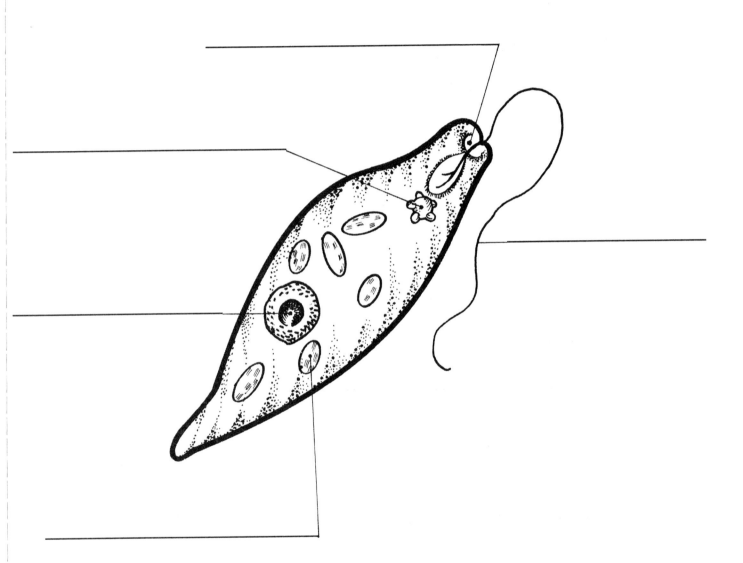

Name_____

The Euglena

Label the parts of a euglena.

| chloroplast | contractile vacuole | eyespot |
| flagellum | nucleus | |

The Paramecium

Label the parts of a reproducing paramecium.

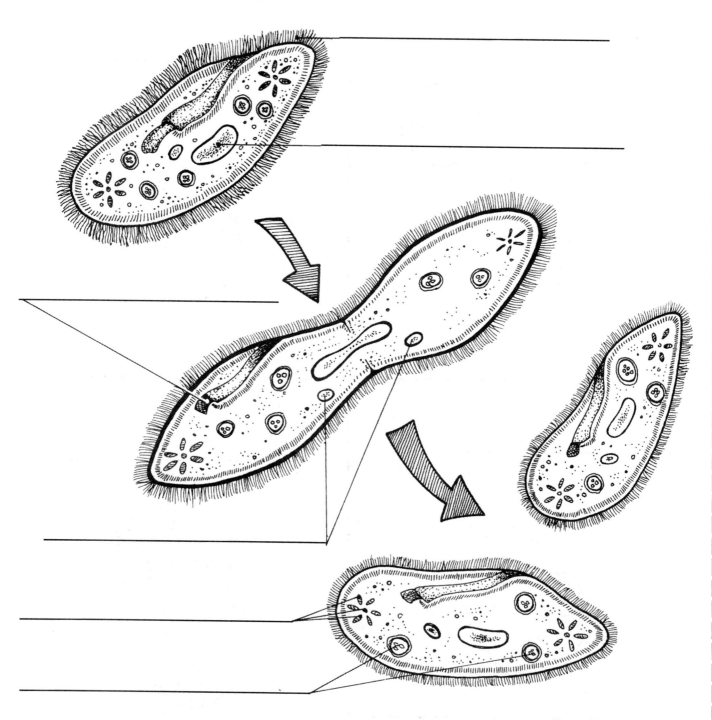

cilia

large nucleus

contractile vacuoles

mouth opening

food vacuoles

small nuclei

The Growth of a Yeast Cell

Label the parts of a growing yeast cell. Then, number the steps in the correct order.

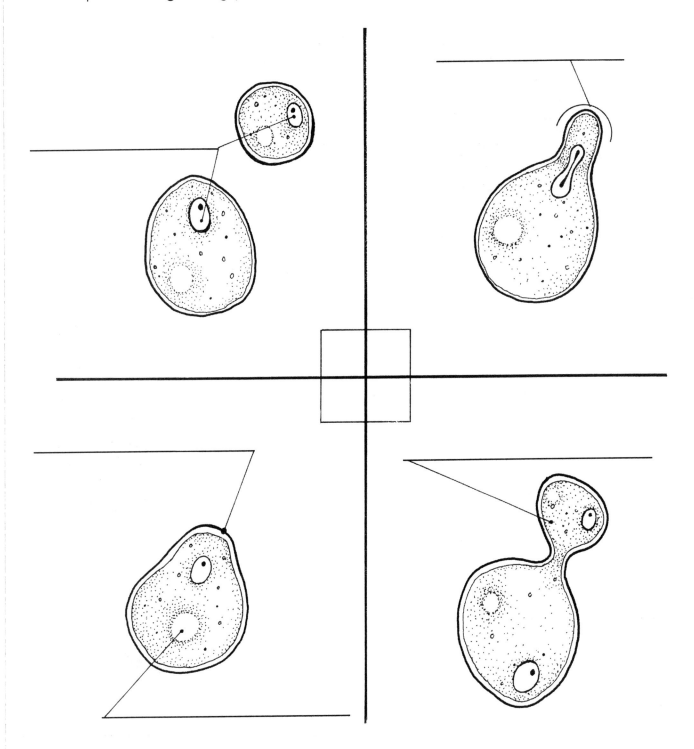

| bud | cell wall | cytoplasm nuclei | nuclei | vacuole |

Food Chains

The organisms found in a typical food chain are pictured. Draw arrows from one organism to the next, showing the order of the food chain. Then, name each organism.

| fish | frog | grass | grasshopper | human |

Find the Missing Link

Write the missing organism in each food chain.

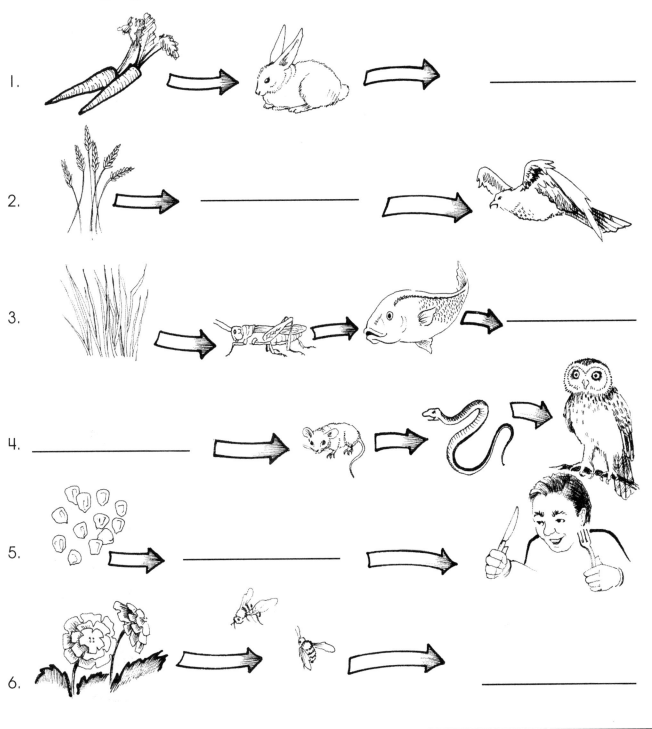

1.

2.

3.

4.

5.

6.

| bear | cow | eagle |
| grass | mouse | skunk |

Producers and Consumers

Organisms are either **producers** or **consumers**, depending on the source of their energy. Producers are organisms that produce their own food, while consumers cannot produce their own food. Consumers are either herbivores, carnivores, or omnivores.

Label the *producer*, *omnivore*, *herbivore*, or *carnivore* in each food chain.

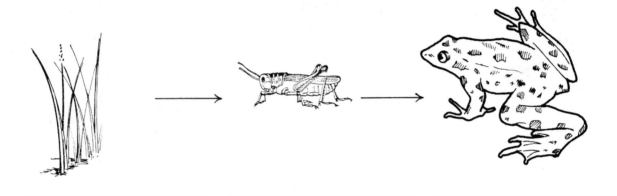

_____   _____   _____

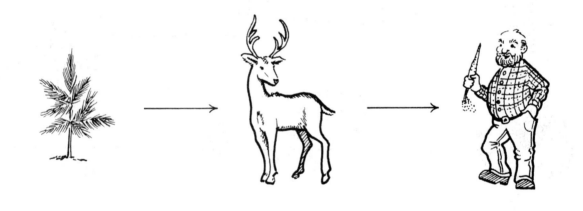

_____   _____   _____

_____   _____   _____

A Food Web

The organisms found in a typical food web are pictured. Use arrows to construct a food web. Then, label the organisms found in the food web.

deer	frog	grass
insect	mouse	raccoon
snake	trout	wolf

An Energy Pyramid

Write the names of the organisms pictured where they belong on the energy pyramid. Some may be listed on more than one level.

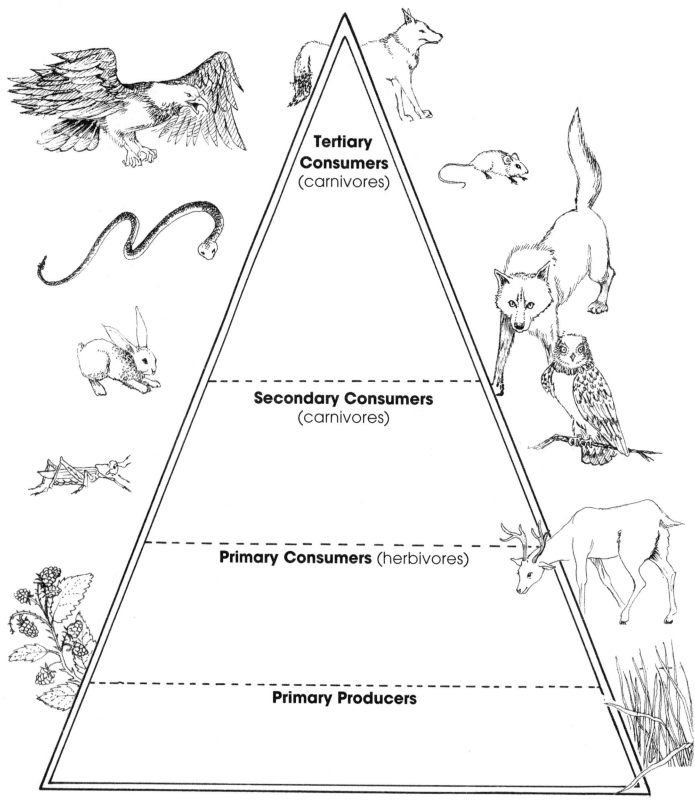

Tertiary Consumers (carnivores)

Secondary Consumers (carnivores)

Primary Consumers (herbivores)

Primary Producers

Biomes of North America

Color the map and key to identify the major biomes of North America.

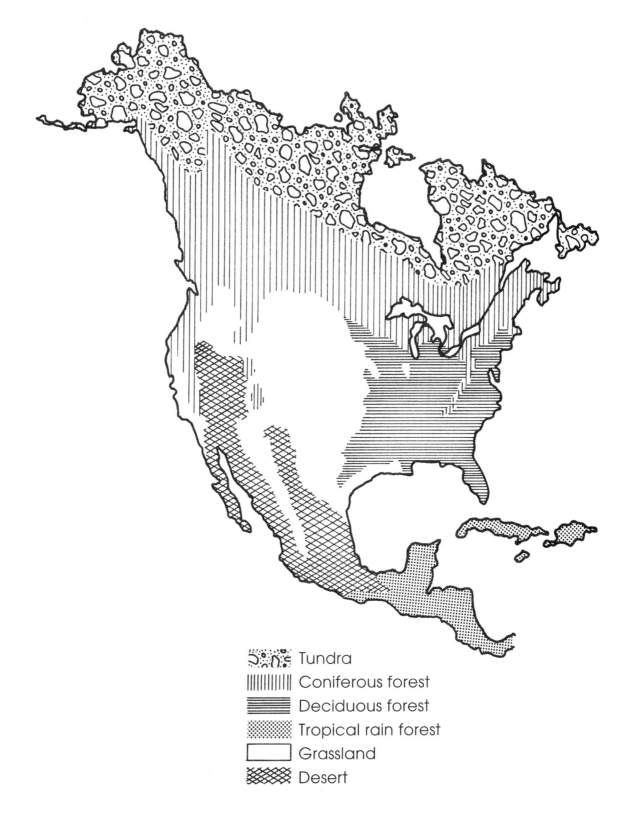

⊙⊙∩⊙ Tundra
|||||||||| Coniferous forest
▬▬▬▬ Deciduous forest
▒▒▒▒ Tropical rain forest
▭ Grassland
▨▨▨▨ Desert

Plant Succession

The slow, gradual change in a community is called **succession**.

Label the different steps of this typical succession. Then, number them in the correct order.

| bog | forest | freshwater pond | meadow |

98   © Carson-Dellosa • CD-104639

Vegetation Layers

Mature forests often have several distinct vertical layers. Each layer supports a different kind of animal life.

Label the five layers of vegetation in the forest shown. Then, list two animals that live in each layer.

_____
1. _____
2. _____

_____
1. _____
2. _____

_____
1. _____
2. _____

1. _____
2. _____

_____
1. _____
2. _____

canopy	forest floor	herb layer
shrub layer	understory	

Laboratory Equipment

Label each piece of laboratory equipment.

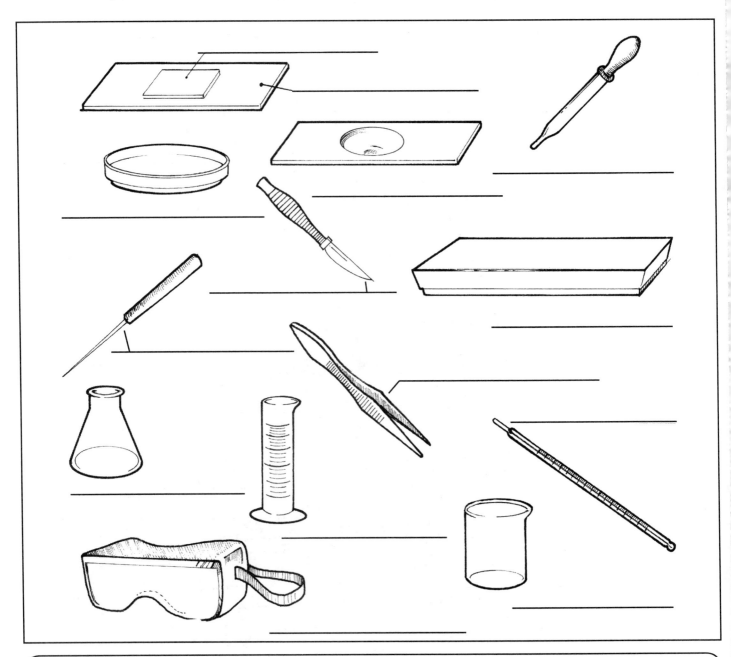

beaker	cover slip	depression slide
dissecting needle	dissecting pan	eyedropper
flask	forceps	glass slide
graduated cylinder	petri dish	safety goggles
scalpel	thermometer	

The Parts of a Compound Microscope

Label the parts of a compound microscope.

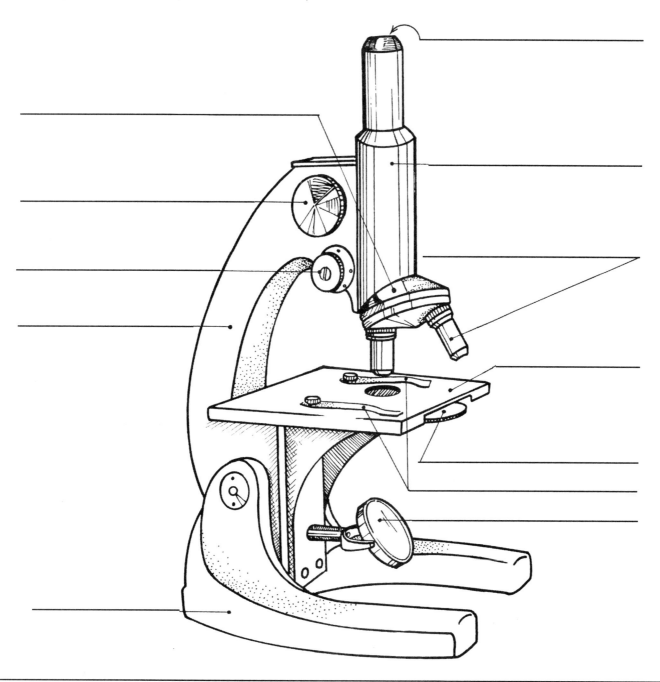

arm	base	body tube
coarse adjustment	diaphragm	eyepiece
fine adjustment	mirror	nosepiece
objective	stage	stage clips

The Parts of a Stereomicroscope

Label the parts of a stereomicroscope.

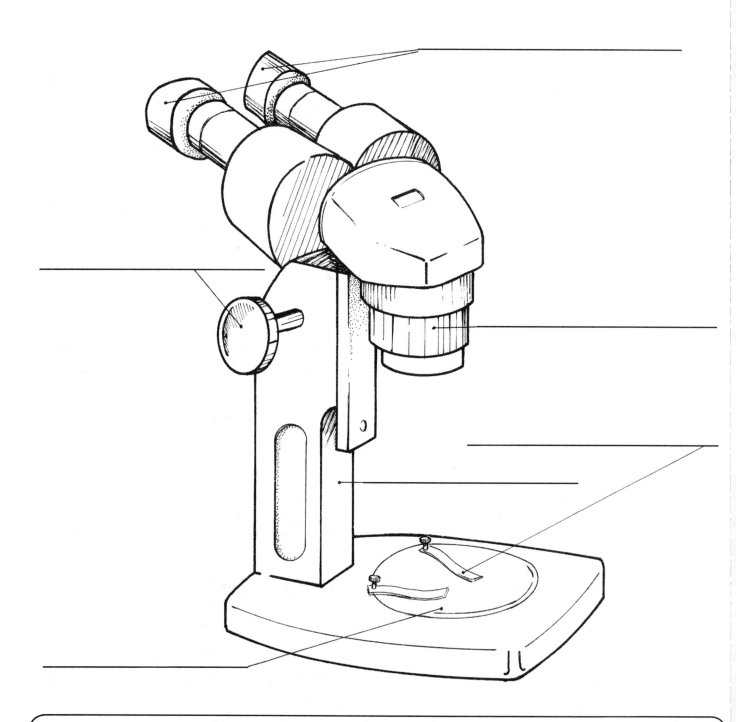

arm	eyepiece	objective lens
single adjustment	stage	stage clip

Answer Key

Name_____

The Five Kingdoms

Scientists have placed all living things into five **kingdoms**. The organisms in each group represent one of the five kingdoms of living things.

Label each kingdom.

protists

fungi

monerans

plants

animals

| animals | fungi | monerans | plants | protists |

© Carson-Dellosa • CD-104639   1

Name_____

Family of Living Things

Scientists divide living things into five main groups called **kingdoms**.

Complete the chart comparing the five kingdoms.

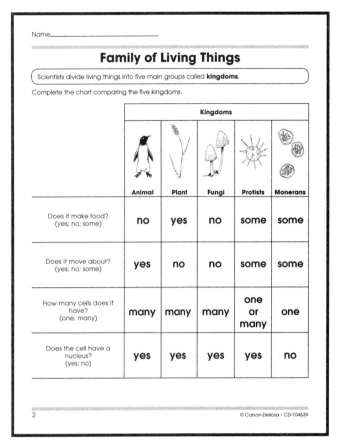

	Kingdoms				
	Animal	Plant	Fungi	Protists	Monerans
Does it make food? (yes; no; some)	no	yes	no	some	some
Does it move about? (yes; no; some)	yes	no	no	some	some
How many cells does it have? (one; many)	many	many	many	one or many	one
Does the cell have a nucleus? (yes; no)	yes	yes	yes	yes	no

2   © Carson-Dellosa • CD-104639

Name_____

Animal or Plant?

Scientists divide all living things into five groups called **kingdoms**. Two of the largest are the animal kingdom and the plant kingdom.

Compare these two kingdoms by using the chart. Check the correct box or boxes next to each characteristic.

Characteristic	Plant	Animal
all living organisms	✓	✓
formed from cells	✓	✓
cells have chlorophyll	✓	
cells have no chlorophyll		✓
makes its own food	✓	
gets food from outside		✓
moves from place to place		✓
has limited movement	✓	
can reproduce its own kind	✓	✓
depends on the sun's energy	✓	✓

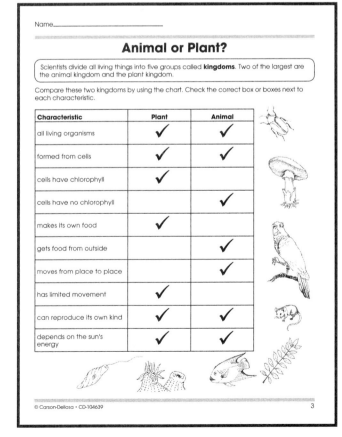

© Carson-Dellosa • CD-104639   3

Name_____

The Plant World

This chart shows how scientists group the different kinds of plants in the plant world.

Place a check in the column(s) that represent the plant with that characteristic.

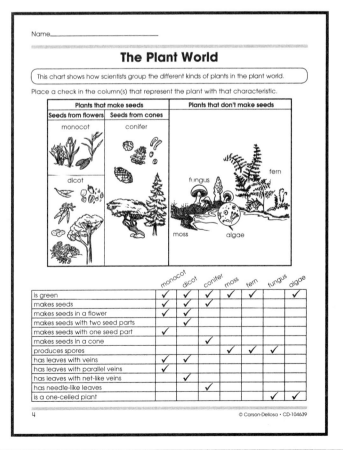

	monocot	dicot	conifer	moss	fern	fungus	algae
is green	✓	✓	✓	✓	✓		✓
makes seeds	✓	✓	✓				
makes seeds in a flower	✓	✓					
makes seeds with two seed parts		✓					
makes seeds with one seed part	✓						
makes seeds in a cone			✓				
produces spores				✓	✓	✓	
has leaves with veins	✓	✓					
has leaves with parallel veins	✓						
has leaves with net-like veins		✓					
has needle-like leaves			✓				
is a one-celled plant						✓	✓

4   © Carson-Dellosa • CD-104639

Answer Key

Plant Parts

Label the parts of a bean plant.

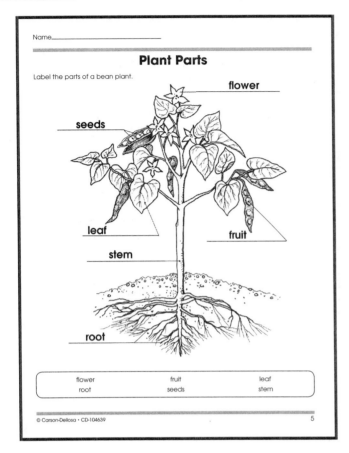

flower · seeds · leaf · stem · root · fruit

| flower | fruit | leaf |
| root | seeds | stem |

A Flowering Plant

Label the parts of a flowering plant.

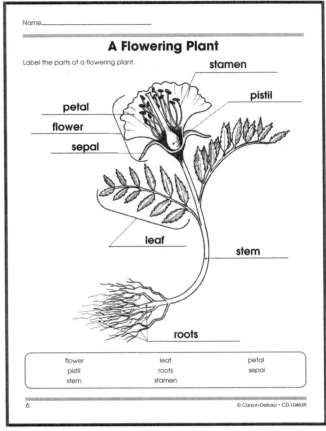

stamen · pistil · petal · flower · sepal · leaf · stem · roots

flower	leaf	petal
pistil	roots	sepal
stem	stamen	

Flower Parts

Label the parts of the two flowers. Some words may be used more than once.

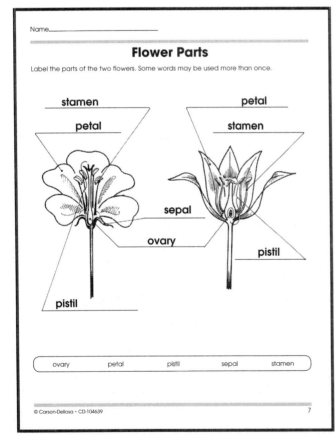

stamen · petal · petal · stamen · sepal · ovary · pistil · pistil

| ovary | petal | pistil | sepal | stamen |

Seed-Producing Parts of a Flower

Label the seed-producting parts of a flower.

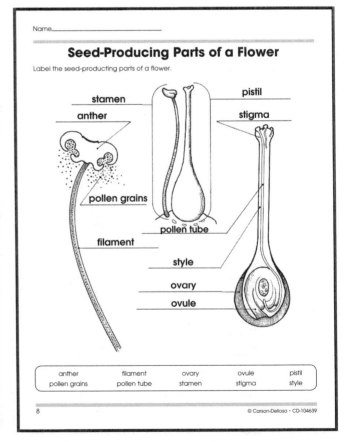

stamen · anther · pollen grains · filament · pistil · stigma · pollen tube · style · ovary · ovule

| anther | filament | ovary | ovule | pistil |
| pollen grains | pollen tube | stamen | stigma | style |

Answer Key

Pollination

Label the main parts involved in each type of pollination.

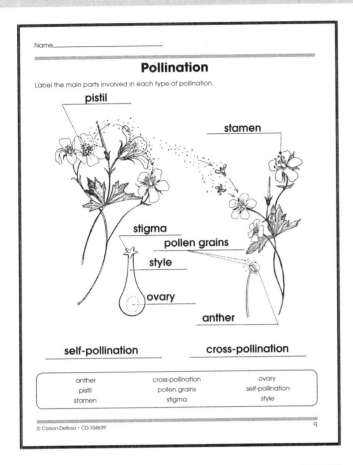

pistil

stamen

stigma

pollen grains

style

ovary

anther

self-pollination   cross-pollination

anther	cross-pollination	ovary
pistil	pollen grains	self-pollination
stamen	stigma	style

Monocot or Dicot?

Describe the characteristic that makes each plant either a dicot or a monocot. Label each plant part either *dicot* or *monocot*.

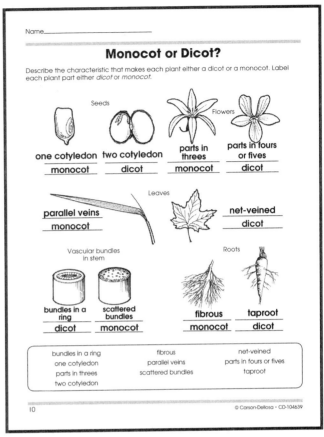

Seeds

one cotyledon   two cotyledon
monocot   dicot

Flowers

parts in threes   parts in fours or fives
monocot   dicot

Leaves

parallel veins
monocot

net-veined
dicot

Vascular bundles in stem

bundles in a ring   scattered bundles
dicot   monocot

Roots

fibrous   taproot
monocot   dicot

bundles in a ring	fibrous	net-veined
one cotyledon	parallel veins	parts in fours or fives
parts in threes	scattered bundles	taproot
two cotyledon		

Eating Plant Parts

Label the edible part of each plant to describe what part of the plant is eaten.

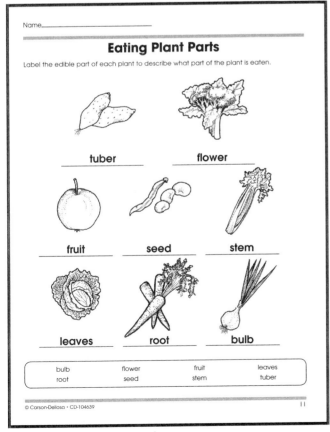

tuber   flower

fruit   seed   stem

leaves   root   bulb

| bulb | flower | fruit | leaves |
| root | seed | stem | tuber |

Corn Grain

Label the parts of a corn grain.

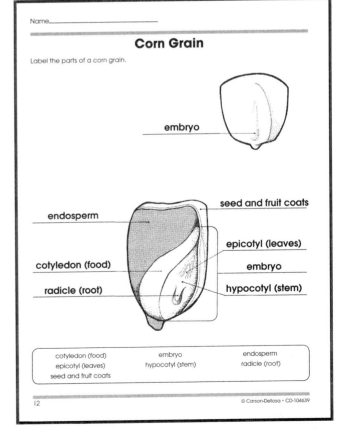

embryo

endosperm

seed and fruit coats

cotyledon (food)

epicotyl (leaves)

radicle (root)

embryo

hypocotyl (stem)

cotyledon (food)	embryo	endosperm
epicotyl (leaves)	hypocotyl (stem)	radicle (root)
seed and fruit coats		

Answer Key

Name_____

Bean Seed

Label the parts of a bean seed.

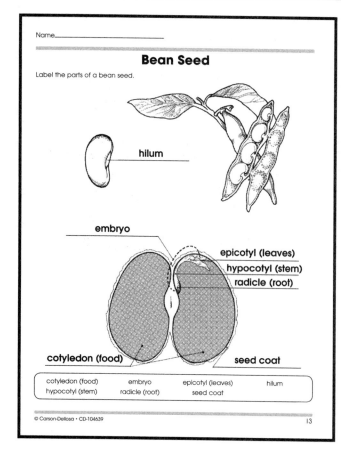

hilum

embryo

epicotyl (leaves)
hypocotyl (stem)
radicle (root)

cotyledon (food)

seed coat

| cotyledon (food) | embryo | epicotyl (leaves) | hilum |
| hypocotyl (stem) | radicle (root) | seed coat | |

© Carson-Dellosa • CD-104639   13

Name_____

Growing Bean Plants

Label the parts of a growing bean plant.

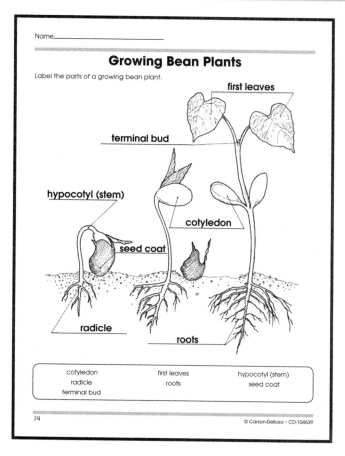

first leaves

terminal bud

hypocotyl (stem)

cotyledon

seed coat

radicle

roots

cotyledon	first leaves	hypocotyl (stem)
radicle	roots	seed coat
terminal bud		

14   © Carson-Dellosa • CD-104639

Name_____

Tropisms

Tropisms occur when plants bend in response to outside stimuli such as light, gravity, or water. Three common types are **geotropism**, which is caused by gravity; **phototropism**, which is caused by light; and **hydrotropism**, which is caused by water.

Label the type of tropism affecting the plant in each picture.

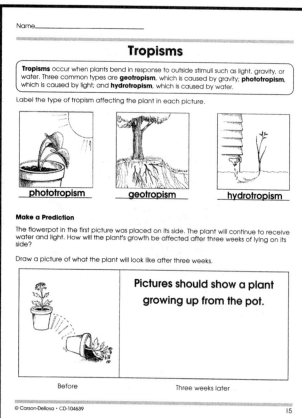

phototropism   geotropism   hydrotropism

Make a Prediction

The flowerpot in the first picture was placed on its side. The plant will continue to receive water and light. How will the plant's growth be affected after three weeks of lying on its side?

Draw a picture of what the plant will look like after three weeks.

Pictures should show a plant growing up from the pot.

Before   Three weeks later

© Carson-Dellosa • CD-104639   15

Name_____

Traveling Seeds

Seeds are dispersed, or scattered, from the parent plant in many ways. The pictures show six examples of how seeds can be dispersed.   **Answers will vary**

Explain how the seeds are being dispersed in each picture.   **but may include:**

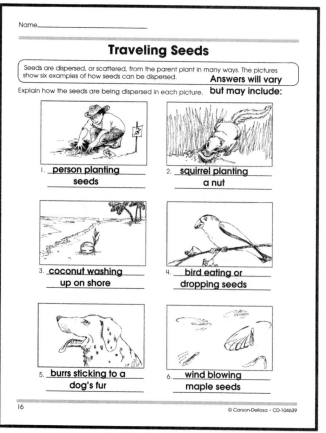

1. person planting seeds
2. squirrel planting a nut
3. coconut washing up on shore
4. bird eating or dropping seeds
5. burrs sticking to a dog's fur
6. wind blowing maple seeds

16   © Carson-Dellosa • CD-104639

Answer Key

Name_____

Parts of a Leaf

Before you can use leaves to help you identify plants, you must know the parts of a leaf. Label the parts of the leaves.

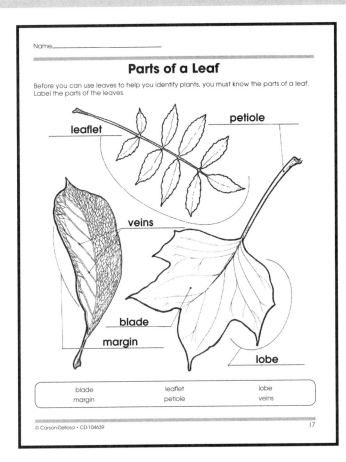

| blade | leaflet | lobe |
| margin | petiole | veins |

Name_____

Leaf Shapes

Label the different characteristics of each group of leaves.

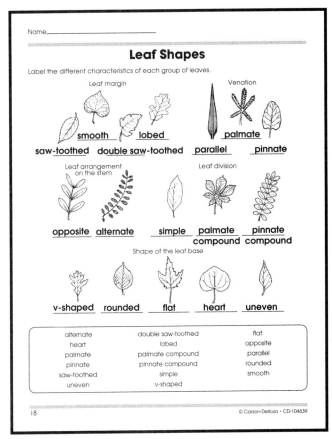

alternate	double saw-toothed	flat
heart	lobed	opposite
palmate	palmate compound	parallel
pinnate	pinnate compound	rounded
saw-toothed	simple	smooth
uneven	v-shaped	

Name_____

Food Factories

Leaves are the "food factories" for green plants. Structures within a leaf change the energy in sunlight into chemical energy that the plant can use as food.

Label the parts of a leaf.

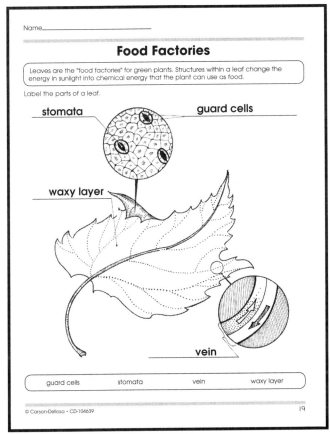

| guard cells | stomata | vein | waxy layer |

Name_____

Leaf Cross Section

Label the parts of the cross section of a leaf.

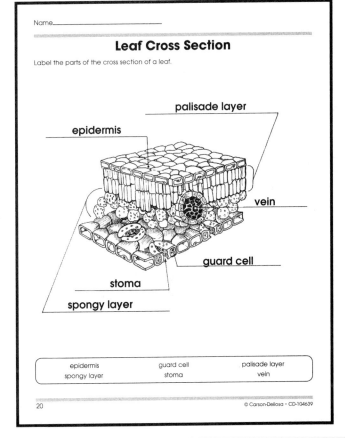

| epidermis | guard cell | palisade layer |
| spongy layer | stoma | vein |

Answer Key

A Key to Trees

A scientist uses a key to identify a tree by its leaves.

Use the following key to identify the leaves pictured.

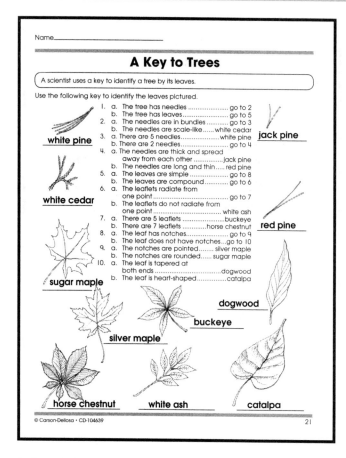

1. a. The tree has needles .... go to 2
   b. The tree has leaves........................ go to 5
2. a. The needles are in bundles .... go to 3
   b. The needles are scale-like......white cedar
3. a. There are 5 needles....................white pine
   b. There are 2 needles..................... go to 4
4. a. The needles are thick and spread
      away from each other ....jack pine
   b. The needles are long and thin..... red pine
5. a. The leaves are simple .... go to 8
   b. The leaves are compound .... go to 6
6. a. The leaflets radiate from
      one point .... go to 7
   b. The leaflets do not radiate from
      one point .... white ash
7. a. There are 5 leaflets ....buckeye
   b. There are 7 leaflets ....horse chestnut
8. a. The leaf has notches...................... go to 9
   b. The leaf does not have notches...go to 10
9. a. The notches are pointed....... silver maple
   b. The notches are rounded..... sugar maple
10. a. The leaf is tapered at
       both ends ....dogwood
    b. The leaf is heart-shaped.............catalpa

white pine

jack pine

white cedar

red pine

sugar maple

dogwood

buckeye

silver maple

horse chestnut

white ash

catalpa

The Tree

Label the three main parts of a tree and the types of tissues in its trunk.

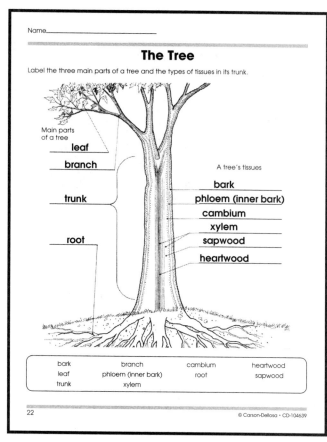

Main parts of a tree

leaf

branch

trunk

root

A tree's tissues

bark

phloem (inner bark)

cambium

xylem

sapwood

heartwood

bark	branch	cambium	heartwood
leaf	phloem (inner bark)	root	sapwood
trunk	xylem		

Tree Stems

Label the parts of a tree stem.

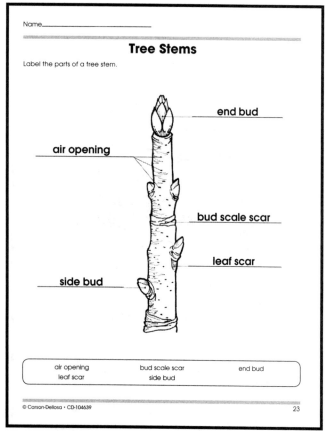

end bud

air opening

bud scale scar

leaf scar

side bud

air opening	bud scale scar	end bud
leaf scar	side bud	

Inside a Tree Trunk

Label the parts of the cross section of a tree trunk. Some words may be used more than once.

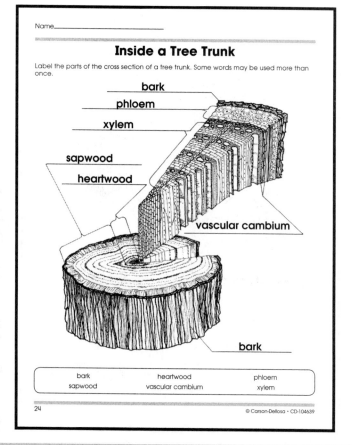

bark

phloem

xylem

sapwood

heartwood

vascular cambium

bark

bark	heartwood	phloem
sapwood	vascular cambium	xylem

Answer Key

Tree History

A freshly cut tree stump can be read like a history book. Label the parts of a tree. Then, study the annual rings, scars, and cuts. Tell what you think happened to the tree.

Tree story:

Answers will vary.

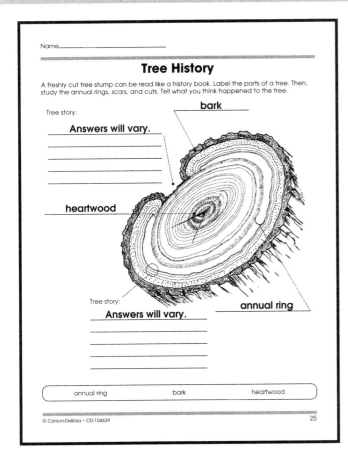

bark

heartwood

annual ring

Tree story:

Answers will vary.

annual ring	bark	heartwood

Underground Stems

Tubers, **rhizomes**, and **bulbs** are three types of underground stems.

Label each type of bulb and its parts. Some words may be used more than once.

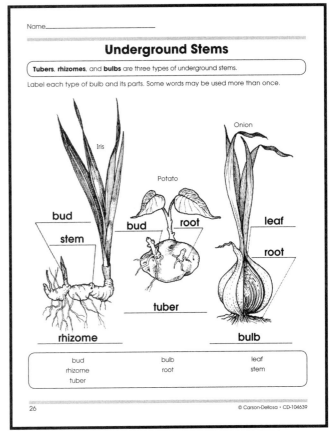

Iris

Onion

Potato

bud

stem

bud

root

leaf

root

rhizome

tuber

bulb

bud	bulb	leaf
rhizome	root	stem
tuber		

Root Systems

Label each root system.

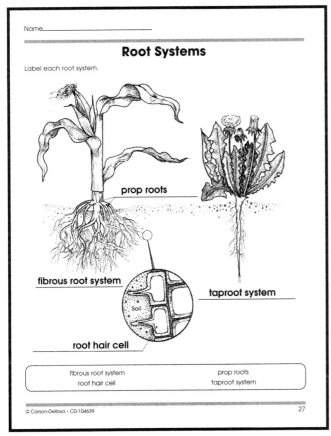

prop roots

fibrous root system

taproot system

Soil

root hair cell

fibrous root system	prop roots
root hair cell	taproot system

Inside a Root

The diagrams show two views of a root. Label both the top cross-sectional and side cross-sectional views.

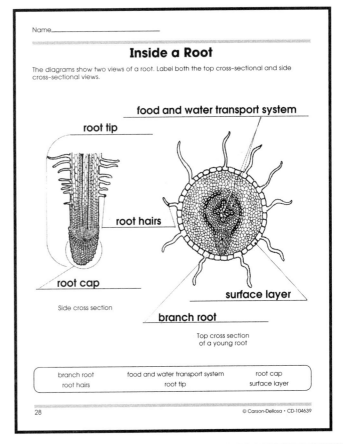

food and water transport system

root tip

root hairs

root cap

Side cross section

surface layer

branch root

Top cross section of a young root

branch root	food and water transport system	root cap
root hairs	root tip	surface layer

Answer Key

Life Cycle of a Conifer

Label the active parts in the life cycle of a conifer tree.

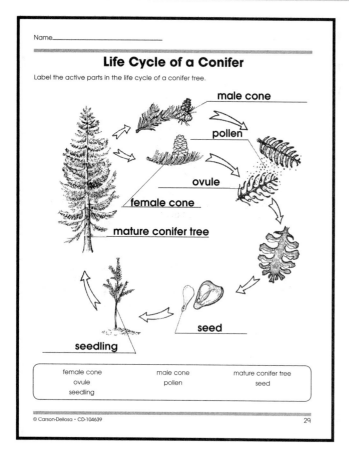

- male cone
- pollen
- ovule
- female cone
- mature conifer tree
- seed
- seedling

female cone	male cone	mature conifer tree
ovule	pollen	seed
seedling		

Ferns

Label the parts of a fern.

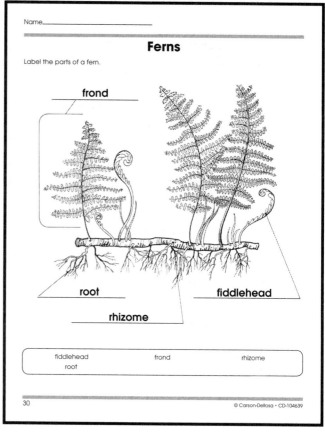

- frond
- root
- fiddlehead
- rhizome

fiddlehead	frond	rhizome
root		

Growth of a Mushroom

Label the parts of a mushroom.

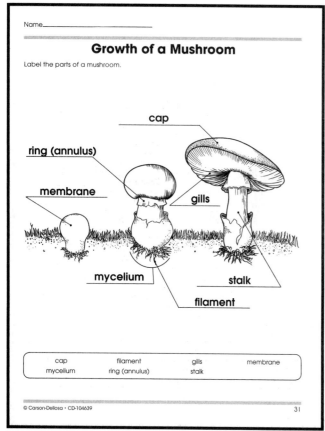

- cap
- ring (annulus)
- membrane
- gills
- mycelium
- stalk
- filament

cap	filament	gills	membrane
mycelium	ring (annulus)	stalk	

Animal Kingdom

The animal kingdom is often divided into subgroups called **phyla**.

Draw a line from each animal to the phylum it belongs in. The, draw a line from each animal to its characteristics.

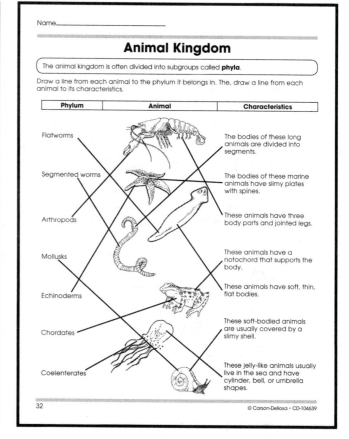

Phylum	Animal	Characteristics
Flatworms		The bodies of these long animals are divided into segments.
Segmented worms		The bodies of these marine animals have slimy plates with spines.
Arthropods		These animals have three body parts and jointed legs.
Mollusks		These animals have a notochord that supports the body.
Echinoderms		These animals have soft, thin, flat bodies.
Chordates		These soft-bodied animals are usually covered by a slimy shell.
Coelenterates		These jelly-like animals usually live in the sea and have cylinder, bell, or umbrella shapes.

Answer Key

Circulatory Systems

The **circulatory system** carries material to every part of the body. It then picks up waste to be removed from the body. Circulatory systems are necessary for continued life in an organism.

Label the parts of the circulatory system for each animal.

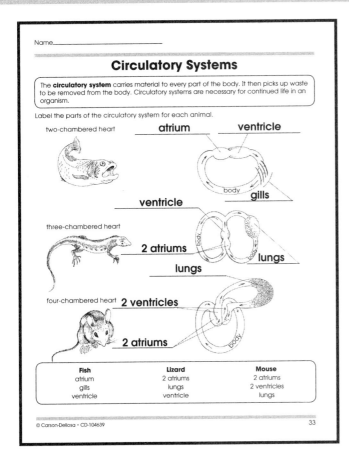

two-chambered heart   **atrium   ventricle**

body   **gills**

three-chambered heart   **ventricle**

2 atriums   lungs

lungs

four-chambered heart   **2 ventricles**

2 atriums   body

Fish	Lizard	Mouse
atrium	2 atriums	2 atriums
gills	lungs	2 ventricles
ventricle	ventricle	lungs

© Carson-Dellosa • CD-104639   33

Animal Defenses

Each of the animals shown has a special defensive adaptation. Name the animal (a). Then, describe its defensive adaptation (b).

a. **turtle**
b. **has a hard shell**

a. **skunk**
b. **sprays pungent odor**

a. **walking stick**
b. **uses camouflage**

a. **ostrich**
b. **long legs for speed and good eyesight**

a. **opossum**
b. **plays dead**

a. **porcupine**
b. **has sharp quills**

opossum	ostrich	porcupine
skunk	turtle	walking stick

34   © Carson-Dellosa • CD-104639

Locomotion

Animals have adaptations that allow them to move from place to place in special ways.

Complete the chart by writing a one-word description of each animal's primary method of moving (locomotion). Then, name the body parts involved in this movement.

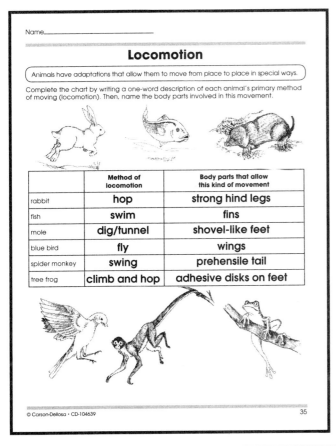

	Method of locomotion	Body parts that allow this kind of movement
rabbit	hop	strong hind legs
fish	swim	fins
mole	dig/tunnel	shovel-like feet
blue bird	fly	wings
spider monkey	swing	prehensile tail
tree frog	climb and hop	adhesive disks on feet

© Carson-Dellosa • CD-104639   35

Symmetrical Critters

There are three types of symmetry: **radial**, **bilateral**, and **asymmetrical**.

After reading the descriptions below, label the type of symmetry each animal has.

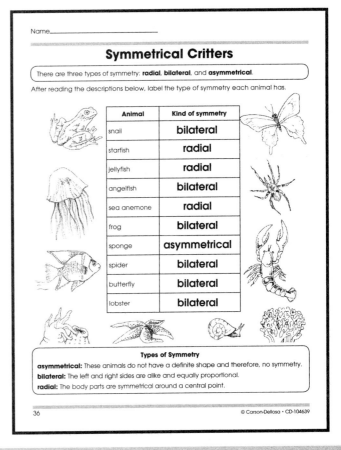

Animal	Kind of symmetry
snail	bilateral
starfish	radial
jellyfish	radial
angelfish	bilateral
sea anemone	radial
frog	bilateral
sponge	asymmetrical
spider	bilateral
butterfly	bilateral
lobster	bilateral

Types of Symmetry

asymmetrical: These animals do not have a definite shape and therefore, no symmetry.
bilateral: The left and right sides are alike and equally proportional.
radial: The body parts are symmetrical around a central point.

36   © Carson-Dellosa • CD-104639

Answer Key

Name_____

Classifying Vertebrates

Vertebrates are sorted into five main groups called **classes**.

Write the name of the class for each vertebrate.

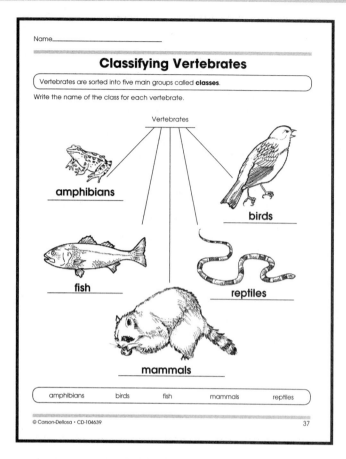

Vertebrates

amphibians

birds

fish

reptiles

mammals

| amphibians | birds | fish | mammals | reptiles |

Name_____

What's a Vertebrate?

Vertebrates are grouped into five different **classes** based on several characteristics. Some classes share characteristics, but they also differ in a few significant ways.

Complete the chart.

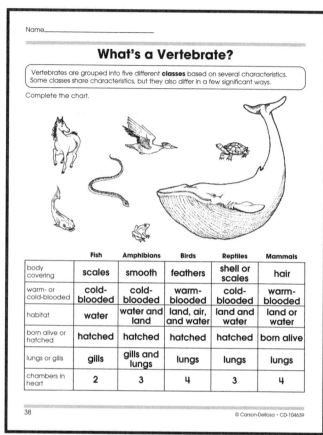

	Fish	Amphibians	Birds	Reptiles	Mammals
body covering	scales	smooth	feathers	shell or scales	hair
warm- or cold-blooded	cold-blooded	cold-blooded	warm-blooded	cold-blooded	warm-blooded
habitat	water	water and land	land, air, and water	land and water	land or water
born alive or hatched	hatched	hatched	hatched	hatched	born alive
lungs or gills	gills	gills and lungs	lungs	lungs	lungs
chambers in heart	2	3	4	3	4

Name_____

Classy Vertebrates

Name the class for each vertebrate. Some words will be used more than once.

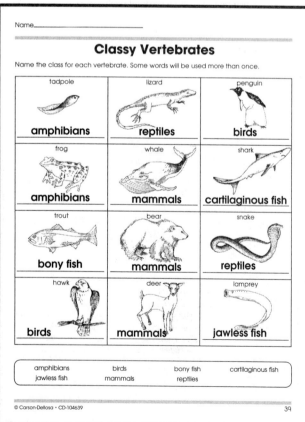

tadpole	lizard	penguin
amphibians	reptiles	birds
frog	whale	shark
amphibians	mammals	cartilaginous fish
trout	bear	snake
bony fish	mammals	reptiles
hawk	deer	lamprey
birds	mammals	jawless fish

| amphibians | birds | bony fish | cartilaginous fish |
| jawless fish | mammals | reptiles | |

Name_____

Animals with Backbones

Vertebrates are animals that have backbones. They are members of a group called **chordates**.

Write the name of the class for each set of characteristics and give an example of each.

Class	Characteristics	Example
cartilaginous fish	—skeleton of cartilage —paired fins —cold-blooded —toothlike scales on skin	shark
jawless fish	—jawless —sucker-shaped mouth —cartilaginous skeleton —cold-blooded	lamprey
bony fish	—skeleton of bone —gill covers —scales —cold-blooded	trout
amphibians	—most young have gills —most adults have lungs —lay eggs in water or moist ground —cold-blooded	frog
reptiles	—dry, scaly skin —egg has tough shell —cold-blooded —well-developed lungs	lizard
birds	—feathers —wings —hollow bones —warm-blooded	hawk
mammals	—have hair at same point in life —feed milk to young —well-developed brain —warm-blooded	bear

amphibians	bear	birds	bony fish	cartilaginous fish
frog	hawk	jawless fish	lamprey	lizard
mammals	reptiles	shark	trout	

Answer Key

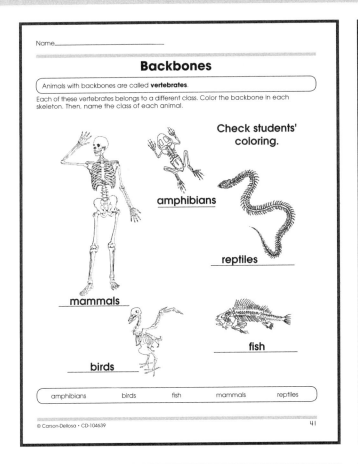

41

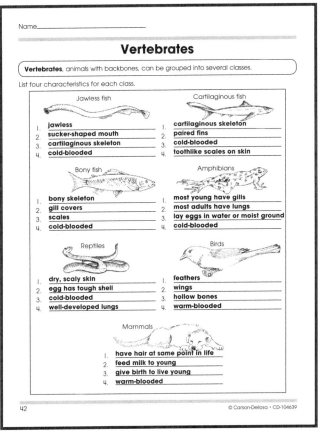

42

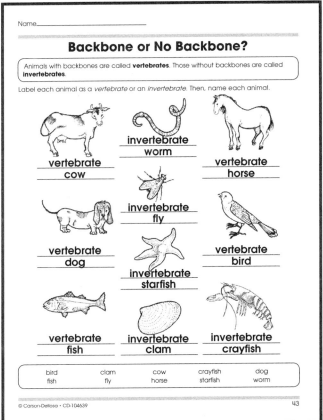

43

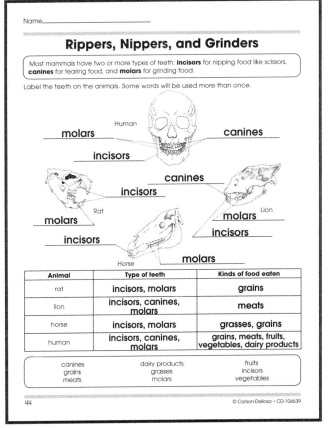

44

Answer Key

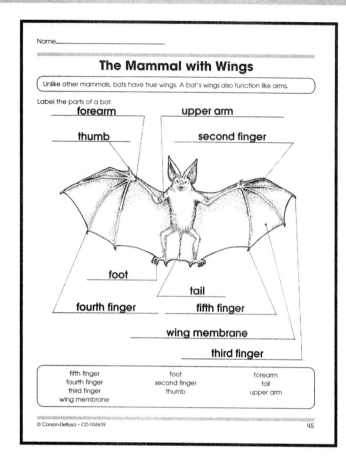
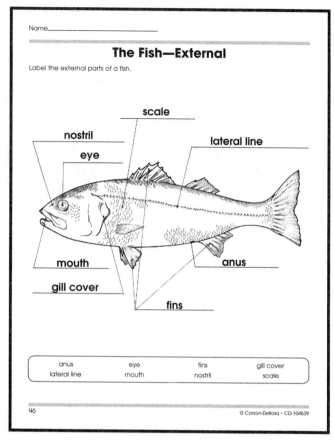
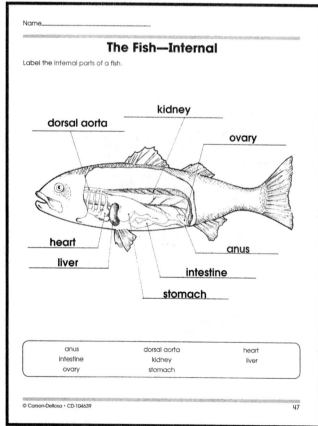
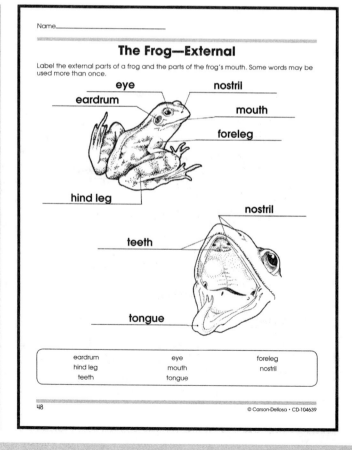

Answer Key

The Frog—Internal

Label the internal parts of a frog.

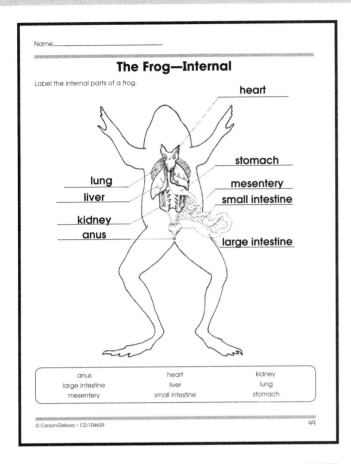

heart

stomach

mesentery

small intestine

lung

liver

kidney

anus

large intestine

anus	heart	kidney
large intestine	liver	lung
mesentery	small intestine	stomach

Life Cycle of a Frog

Label the steps in the life cycle of a frog.

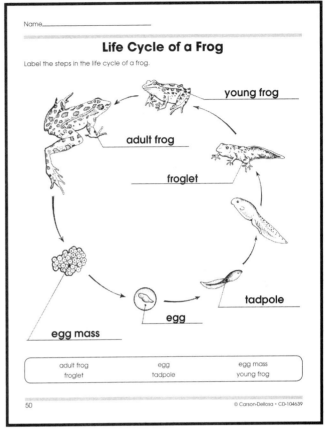

young frog

adult frog

froglet

tadpole

egg

egg mass

adult frog	egg	egg mass
froglet	tadpole	young frog

Pit Viper

Label the parts of the head of a pit viper.

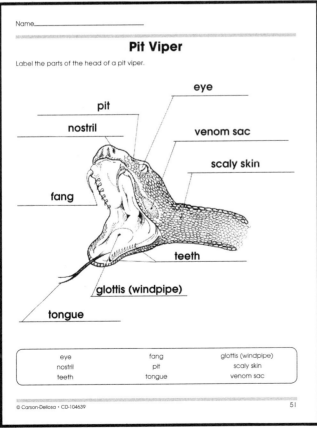

eye

pit

nostril

venom sac

scaly skin

fang

teeth

glottis (windpipe)

tongue

eye	fang	glottis (windpipe)
nostril	pit	scaly skin
teeth	tongue	venom sac

The Bird

Label the parts of a bird.

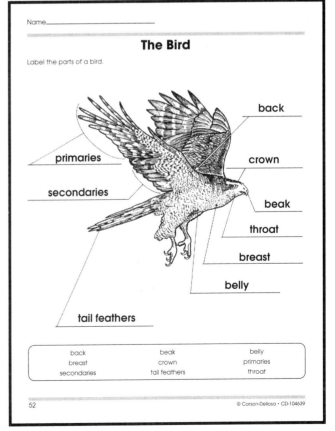

back

crown

primaries

beak

secondaries

throat

breast

belly

tail feathers

back	beak	belly
breast	crown	primaries
secondaries	tail feathers	throat

Answer Key

Feathers and Wings

The wings and body of a bird are covered with different types of feathers.

Parts of a Wing

Label the three groups of feathers on the wing.

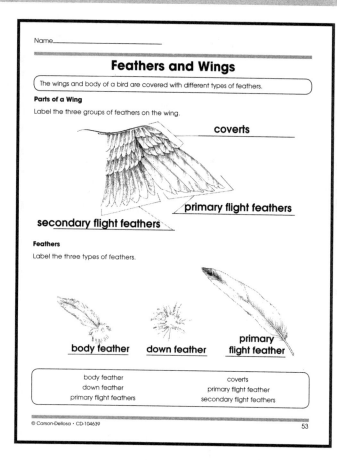

coverts

primary flight feathers

secondary flight feathers

Feathers

Label the three types of feathers.

body feather   down feather   primary flight feather

body feather	coverts
down feather	primary flight feather
primary flight feathers	secondary flight feathers

© Carson-Dellosa • CD-104639   53

Bird Bones

Label the major bone structures of a bird.

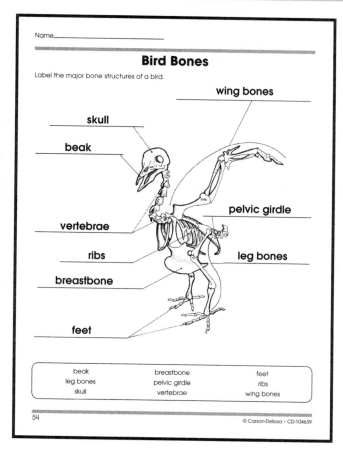

wing bones

skull

beak

pelvic girdle

vertebrae

ribs   leg bones

breastbone

feet

beak	breastbone	feet
leg bones	pelvic girdle	ribs
skull	vertebrae	wing bones

54   © Carson-Dellosa • CD-104639

Feathered Friends' Feet

A bird's feet can tell you many things about its habits or home.

Tell how each bird uses its feet.

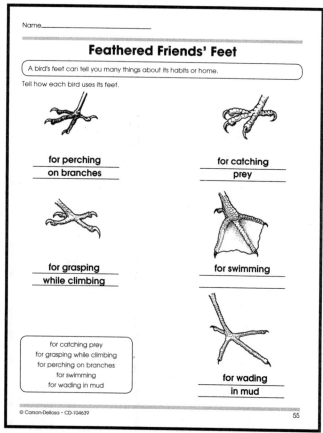

for perching
on branches

for catching
prey

for grasping
while climbing

for swimming

for wading
in mud

for catching prey
for grasping while climbing
for perching on branches
for swimming
for wading in mud

© Carson-Dellosa • CD-104639   55

Bird Beaks

The shape of a bird's beak will often tell you what the bird eats.

Tell how each bird uses its beak to eat food.

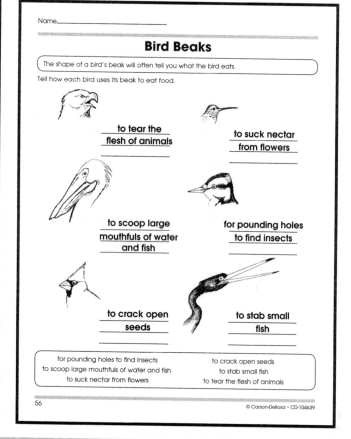

to tear the
flesh of animals

to suck nectar
from flowers

to scoop large
mouthfuls of water
and fish

for pounding holes
to find insects

to crack open
seeds

to stab small
fish

for pounding holes to find insects
to scoop large mouthfuls of water and fish
to suck nectar from flowers
to crack open seeds
to stab small fish
to tear the flesh of animals

56   © Carson-Dellosa • CD-104639

© Carson-Dellosa • CD-104639

Answer Key

More Bird Beaks

The shape of a bird's beak will often tell what kind of food the bird eats.

Describe the feeding habits of each bird.

scoops fish from water

tears flesh

cracks nuts and seeds

traps insects in midair

grabs and holds worms

sweeps back and forth through water and filters out tiny plants and animals

cracks nuts and seeds
scoops fish from water
tears flesh

grabs and holds worms
sweeps back and forth through water to filter out tiny plants and animals
traps insects in midair

© Carson-Dellosa • CD-104639   57

Name

Strangers in the Night

It is much easier to identify a bird when you can see its coloring, size, and shape. At night, this is usually difficult.

Identify each bird by its silhouette.

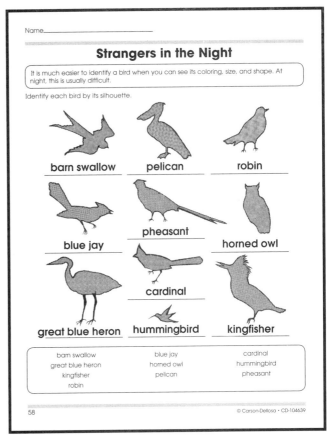

barn swallow   pelican   robin

blue jay   pheasant   horned owl

great blue heron   cardinal   hummingbird   kingfisher

barn swallow   blue jay   cardinal
great blue heron   horned owl   hummingbird
kingfisher   pelican   pheasant
robin

58   © Carson-Dellosa • CD-104639

Name

Highways for the Birds

A **flyway** is the path that migrating birds will follow, often traveling great distances.

Label each of the major flyways found in North America.

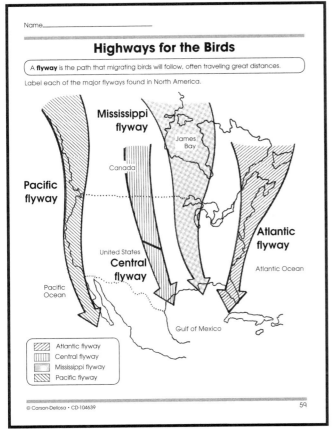

Mississippi flyway

James Bay

Canada

Pacific flyway

Atlantic flyway

Pacific Ocean

United States

Central flyway

Atlantic Ocean

Pacific Ocean

Gulf of Mexico

Atlantic flyway
Central flyway
Mississippi flyway
Pacific flyway

© Carson-Dellosa • CD-104639   59

Name

Bird Eggs

Label the parts of an egg.

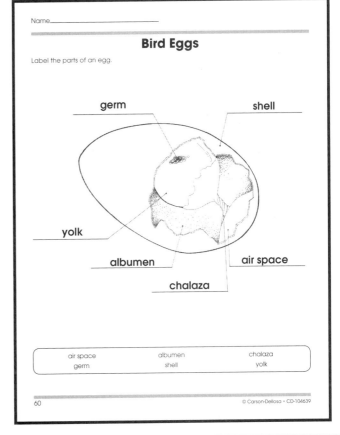

germ   shell

yolk

albumen   air space

chalaza

air space   albumen   chalaza
germ   shell   yolk

60   © Carson-Dellosa • CD-104639

Answer Key

Name

Chicken Eggs

Label the parts of a fertilized hen's egg.

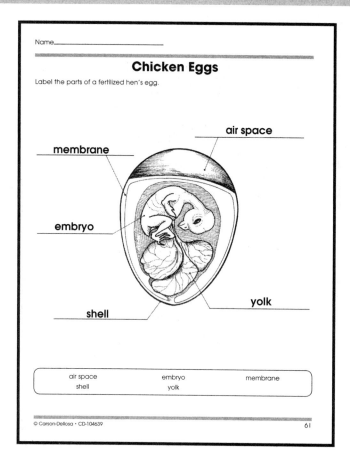

air space

membrane

embryo

shell

yolk

| air space | embryo | membrane |
| shell | yolk | |

61

Name

Classes of Arthropods

Arthropods are animals that have jointed legs. Three-fourths of all of the different animal types belong to this group.

Write the name of the class for each set of characteristics and give an example of each.

Class	Characteristics	Example
Diplopoda	—round —segmented body —two pairs of legs per segment	millipede
Chilopoda	—flat —segmented body —one pair of legs per segment	centipede
Crustacea	—hard —flexible exoskeleton —gills —two pairs of antennae —two body sections	lobster
Arachnida	—two body sections —no antennae —four pairs of legs	spider
Insecta	—three body sections —one pair of antennae —three pairs of legs	bee

Arachnida	bee	centipede
Chilopoda	Crustacea	Diplopoda
Insecta	lobster	millipede
spider		

62

Name

The Crayfish

Label the parts of a crayfish.

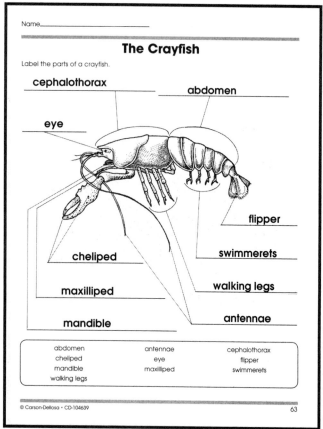

cephalothorax

abdomen

eye

flipper

swimmerets

cheliped

walking legs

maxilliped

antennae

mandible

abdomen	antennae	cephalothorax
cheliped	eye	flipper
mandible	maxilliped	swimmerets
walking legs		

63

Name

Insect Orders

The major groups of insects are called **orders**. Below are examples from seven of the most common orders of insects.

Label each insect and its order.

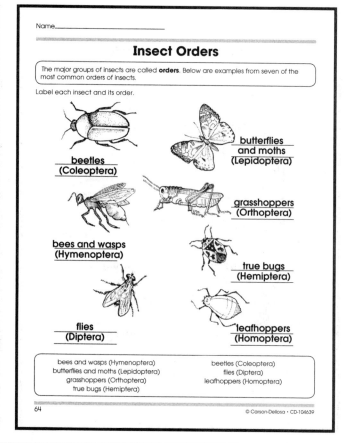

beetles (Coleoptera)

butterflies and moths (Lepidoptera)

bees and wasps (Hymenoptera)

grasshoppers (Orthoptera)

true bugs (Hemiptera)

flies (Diptera)

leafhoppers (Homoptera)

bees and wasps (Hymenoptera)	beetles (Coleoptera)
butterflies and moths (Lepidoptera)	flies (Diptera)
grasshoppers (Orthoptera)	leafhoppers (Homoptera)
true bugs (Hemiptera)	

64

Answer Key

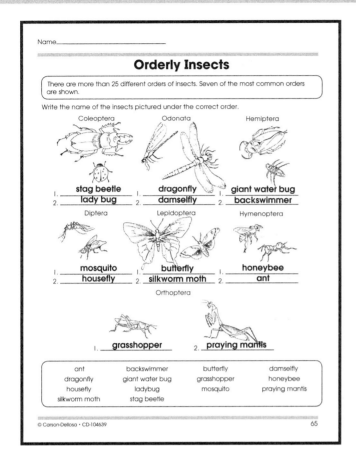

Name_____

Orderly Insects

There are more than 25 different orders of insects. Seven of the most common orders are shown.

Write the name of the insects pictured under the correct order.

Coleoptera   Odonata   Hemiptera

1. stag beetle
2. lady bug

1. dragonfly
2. damselfly

1. giant water bug
2. backswimmer

Diptera   Lepidoptera   Hymenoptera

1. mosquito
2. housefly

1. butterfly
2. silkworm moth

1. honeybee
2. ant

Orthoptera

1. grasshopper   2. praying mantis

ant	backswimmer	butterfly	damselfly
dragonfly	giant water bug	grasshopper	honeybee
housefly	ladybug	mosquito	praying mantis
silkworm moth	stag beetle		

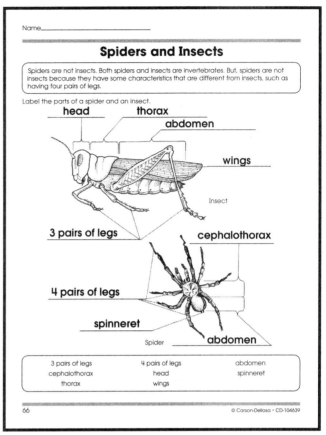

Name_____

Spiders and Insects

Spiders are not insects. Both spiders and insects are invertebrates. But, spiders are not insects because they have some characteristics that are different from insects, such as having four pairs of legs.

Label the parts of a spider and an insect.

head   thorax
abdomen
wings

Insect

3 pairs of legs   cephalothorax

4 pairs of legs

spinneret

Spider   abdomen

3 pairs of legs	4 pairs of legs	abdomen
cephalothorax	head	spinneret
thorax	wings	

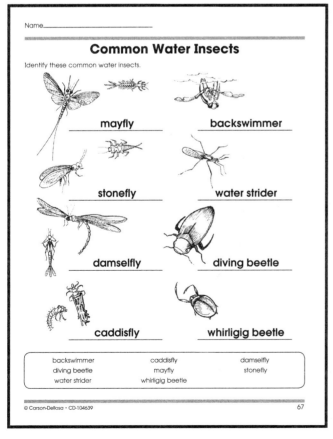

Name_____

Common Water Insects

Identify these common water insects.

mayfly   backswimmer

stonefly   water strider

damselfly   diving beetle

caddisfly   whirligig beetle

backswimmer	caddisfly	damselfly
diving beetle	mayfly	stonefly
water strider	whirligig beetle	

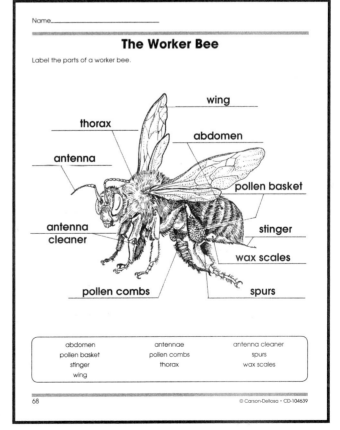

Name_____

The Worker Bee

Label the parts of a worker bee.

wing
thorax
abdomen
antenna
pollen basket
antenna cleaner
stinger
wax scales
pollen combs   spurs

abdomen	antennae	antenna cleaner
pollen basket	pollen combs	spurs
stinger	thorax	wax scales
wing		

Answer Key

The Life Cycle of a Bee

Label the stages of a bee's life cycle.

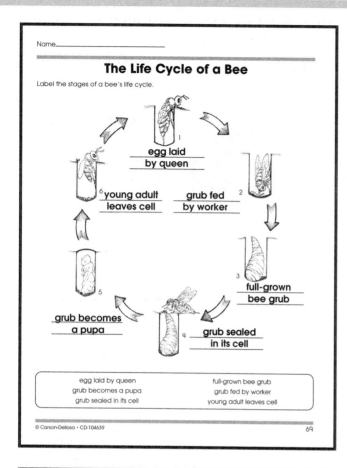

egg laid by queen	full-grown bee grub
grub becomes a pupa	grub fed by worker
grub sealed in its cell	young adult leaves cell

The Ant

Label the parts of an ant's body.

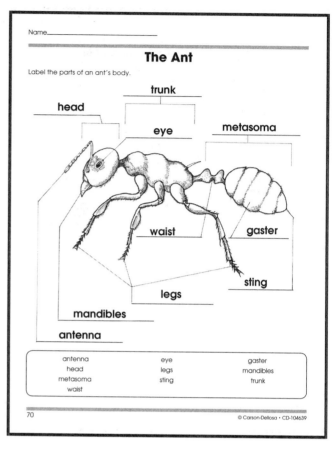

antenna	eye	gaster
head	legs	mandibles
metasoma	sting	trunk
waist		

The Life Cycle of an Ant

Label the stages of an ant's life cycle.

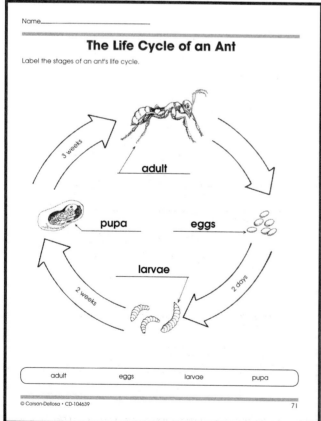

adult	eggs	larvae	pupa

The Grasshopper

Label the parts of a grasshopper.

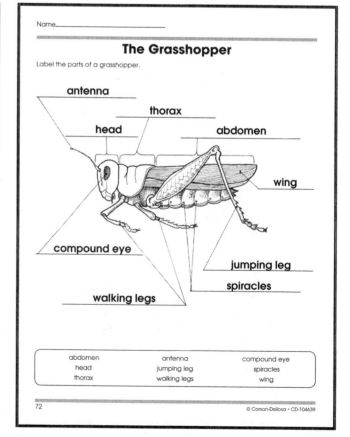

abdomen	antenna	compound eye
head	jumping leg	spiracles
thorax	walking legs	wing

Answer Key

The Grasshopper's Life Cycle

The grasshopper's life cycle is an example of **gradual metamorphosis**. Gradual metamorphosis in insects is where the immature stages are similar in appearance to the adult stage, except smaller and without reproductive capabilities. It is also referred to as **simple metamorphosis**.

Label the stages of a grasshopper's life cycle.

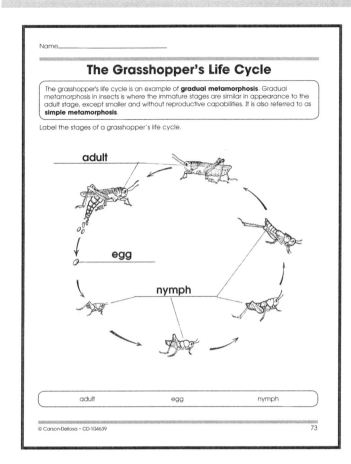

adult	egg	nymph

73

Butterflies and Moths

Butterflies and moths belong to the order of insects called Lepidoptera. Moths and butterflies each have special characteristics to help you tell them apart.

Label the parts of the butterfly. Then, label the special characteristics as either *butterfly* or *moth*.

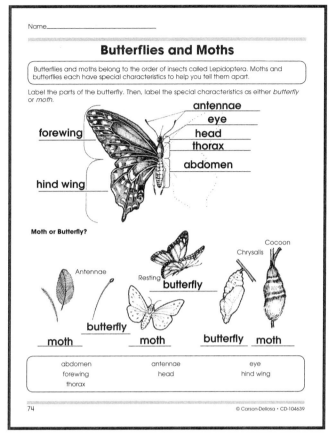

Moth or Butterfly?

abdomen	antennae	eye
forewing	head	hind wing
thorax		

74

The Monarch's Life Cycle

The life cycle of a monarch butterfly is an example of **complete metamorphosis**. Complete metamorphosis is when an insect passes through four separate stages of growth: egg, larva, pupa, and adult. Each stage looks distinct.

Label the stages of a monarch butterfly's life cycle.

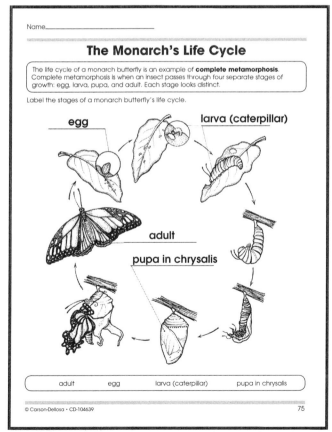

adult	egg	larva (caterpillar)	pupa in chrysalis

75

Metamorphosis

Label the stages of complete and incomplete metamorphosis. Some words may be used more than once.

Complete Metamorphosis

Incomplete Metamorphosis

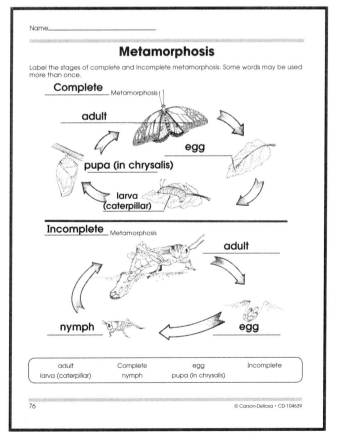

adult	Complete	egg	Incomplete
larva (caterpillar)	nymph	pupa (in chrysalis)	

76

Answer Key

The Clam

Label the parts of a clam.

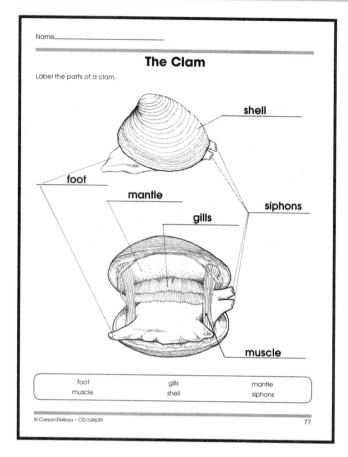

shell

foot

mantle

siphons

gills

muscle

foot	gills	mantle
muscle	shell	siphons

77

The Starfish

Label the parts of a starfish.

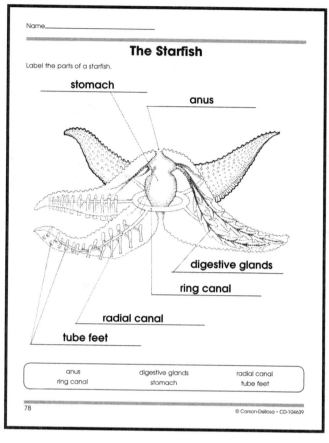

stomach

anus

digestive glands

ring canal

radial canal

tube feet

anus	digestive glands	radial canal
ring canal	stomach	tube feet

78

The Sponge

Label the parts of a sponge.

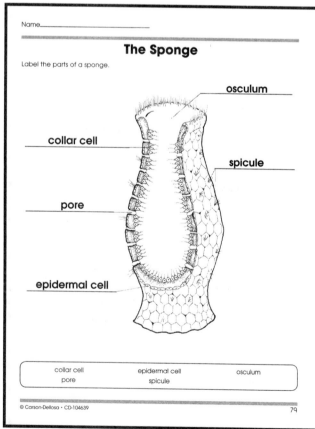

osculum

collar cell

spicule

pore

epidermal cell

collar cell	epidermal cell	osculum
pore	spicule	

79

The Hydra

Label the parts of a hydra.

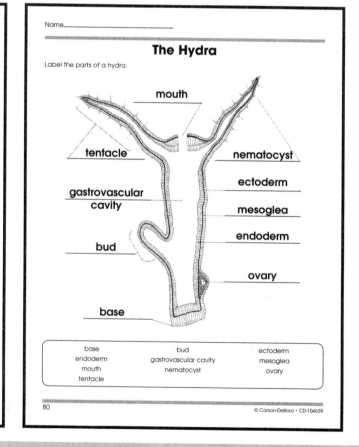

mouth

tentacle

nematocyst

gastrovascular cavity

ectoderm

mesoglea

endoderm

bud

ovary

base

base	bud	ectoderm
endoderm	gastrovascular cavity	mesoglea
mouth	nematocyst	ovary
tentacle		

80

Answer Key

The Planarian

A **planarian** is a small flatworm that can regenerate missing body parts when portions are cut off.

Label the parts of the regenerated planarian.

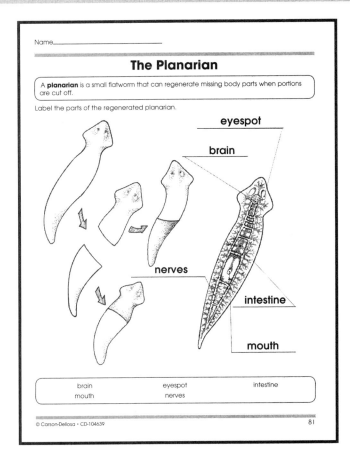

eyespot

brain

nerves

intestine

mouth

brain	eyespot	intestine
mouth	nerves	

Worms

There are thousands of different kinds of worms. Each kind belongs to one of the four major groups of worms.

Draw a line from each worm to the group to which it belongs.

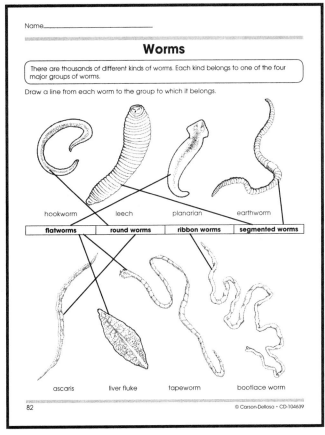

hookworm   leech   planarian   earthworm

flatworms	round worms	ribbon worms	segmented worms

ascaris   liver fluke   tapeworm   bootlace worm

More Worms

A **key** is a tool used by scientists to help them identify living things.

Use the key to identify each worm.

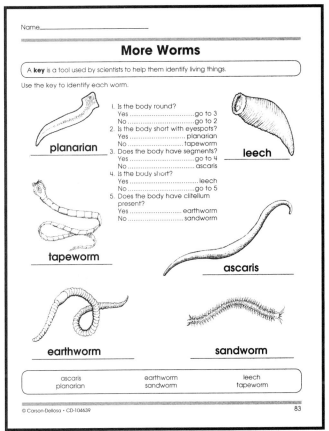

1. Is the body round?
   Yes ....go to 3
   No ....go to 2
2. Is the body short with eyespots?
   Yes .... planarian
   No .... tapeworm
3. Does the body have segments?
   Yes ....go to 4
   No ....ascaris
4. Is the body short?
   Yes ....leech
   No ....go to 5
5. Does the body have clitellum present?
   Yes .... earthworm
   No .... sandworm

planarian

leech

tapeworm

ascaris

earthworm

sandworm

ascaris	earthworm	leech
planarian	sandworm	tapeworm

The Earthworm

Label the external parts of an earthworm.

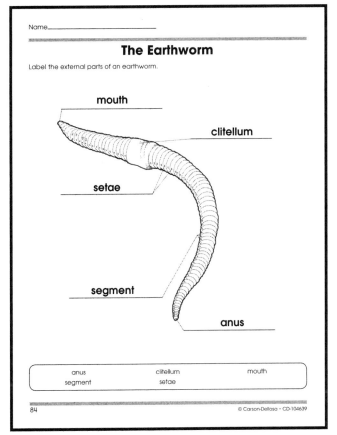

mouth

clitellum

setae

segment

anus

anus	clitellum	mouth
segment	setae	

Answer Key

The Earthworm's Circulatory System

The earthworm's circulatory system is very simple.

Label the parts of an earthworm and its circulatory system.

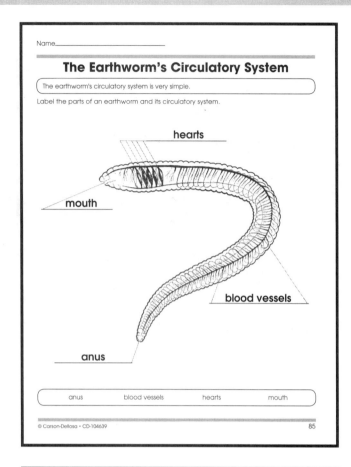

hearts

mouth

blood vessels

anus

| anus | blood vessels | hearts | mouth |

The Earthworm's Digestive System

In the earthworm, as in most animals, digestion takes place in a long tube with openings at both ends. This tube is divided into organs that have different jobs.

Label the parts of an earthworm's digestive system.

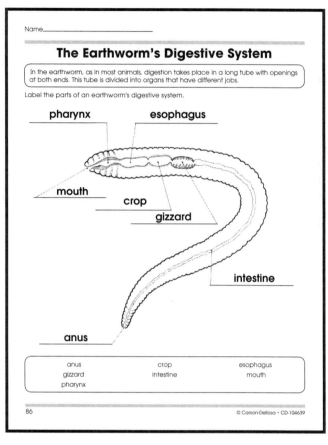

pharynx

esophagus

mouth

crop

gizzard

intestine

anus

anus	crop	esophagus
gizzard	intestine	mouth
pharynx		

Plant and Animal Cells

Plant and animal cells are alike in many ways. But, there are also ways in which they differ. Label the parts of the plant and animal cells. Some words may be used more than once.

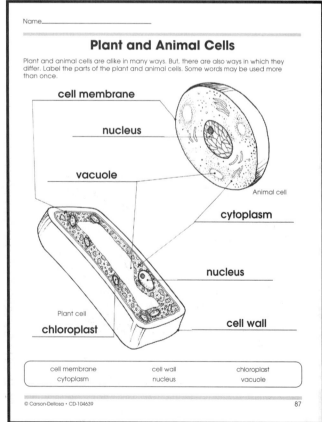

cell membrane

nucleus

vacuole

Animal cell

cytoplasm

nucleus

Plant cell

cell wall

chloroplast

| cell membrane | cell wall | chloroplast |
| cytoplasm | nucleus | vacuole |

The Amoeba

Label the parts of a reproducing amoeba.

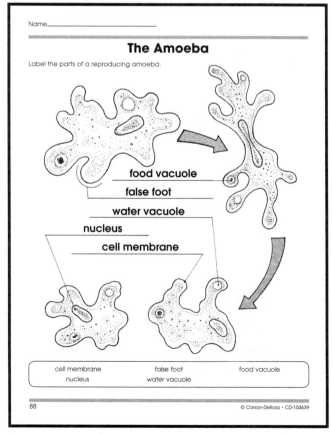

food vacuole

false foot

water vacuole

nucleus

cell membrane

| cell membrane | false foot | food vacuole |
| nucleus | water vacuole | |

Answer Key

Name_____

The Euglena

Label the parts of a euglena.

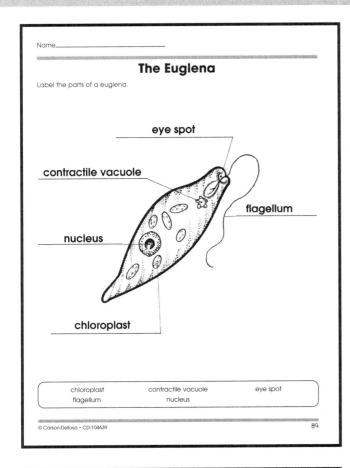

- eye spot
- contractile vacuole
- flagellum
- nucleus
- chloroplast

| chloroplast | contractile vacuole | eye spot |
| flagellum | nucleus | |

Name_____

The Paramecium

Label the parts of a reproducing paramecium.

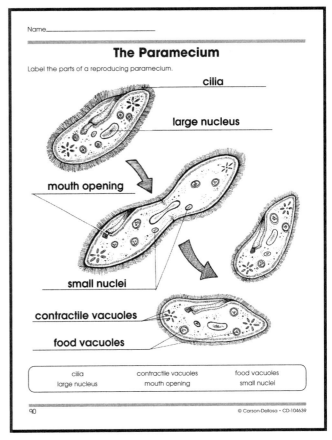

- cilia
- large nucleus
- mouth opening
- small nuclei
- contractile vacuoles
- food vacuoles

| cilia | contractile vacuoles | food vacuoles |
| large nucleus | mouth opening | small nuclei |

Name_____

The Growth of a Yeast Cell

Label the parts of a growing yeast cell. Then, number the steps in the correct order.

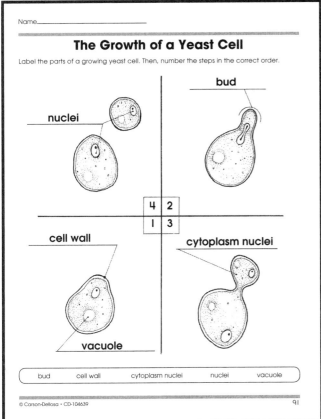

- bud
- nuclei
- cell wall
- cytoplasm nuclei
- vacuole

| 4 | 2 |
| 1 | 3 |

| bud | cell wall | cytoplasm nuclei | nuclei | vacuole |

Name_____

Food Chains

The organisms found in a typical food chain are pictured. Draw arrows from one organism to the next, showing the order of the food chain. Then, name each organism.

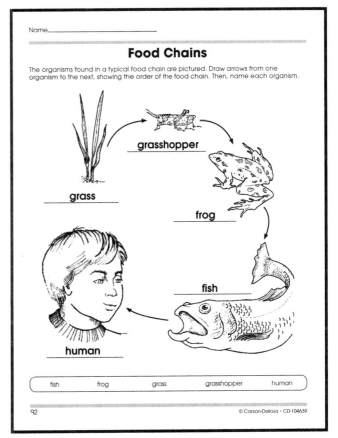

- grasshopper
- grass
- frog
- fish
- human

| fish | frog | grass | grasshopper | human |

Answer Key

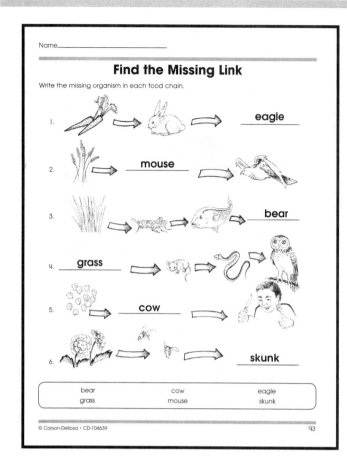

Find the Missing Link

Write the missing organism in each food chain.

1. carrot → rabbit → eagle
2. grass → __mouse__ → eagle
3. grass → __bear__
4. __grass__ → mouse → snake → owl
5. corn → __cow__ → boy
6. flower → bee → __skunk__

| bear | cow | eagle |
| grass | mouse | skunk |

© Carson-Dellosa • CD-104639   93

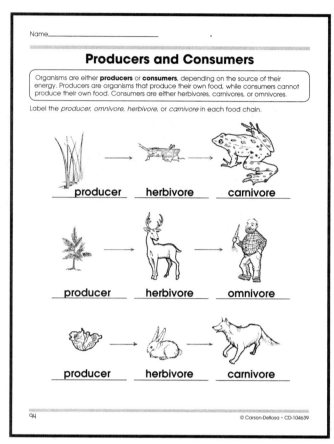

Producers and Consumers

Organisms are either **producers** or **consumers**, depending on the source of their energy. Producers are organisms that produce their own food, while consumers cannot produce their own food. Consumers are either herbivores, carnivores, or omnivores.

Label the *producer, omnivore, herbivore,* or *carnivore* in each food chain.

__producer__   __herbivore__   __carnivore__

__producer__   __herbivore__   __omnivore__

__producer__   __herbivore__   __carnivore__

94   © Carson-Dellosa • CD-104639

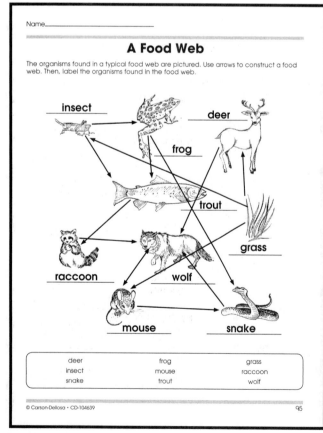

A Food Web

The organisms found in a typical food web are pictured. Use arrows to construct a food web. Then, label the organisms found in the food web.

insect   deer
frog
trout
grass
raccoon   wolf
mouse   snake

deer	frog	grass
insect	mouse	raccoon
snake	trout	wolf

© Carson-Dellosa • CD-104639   95

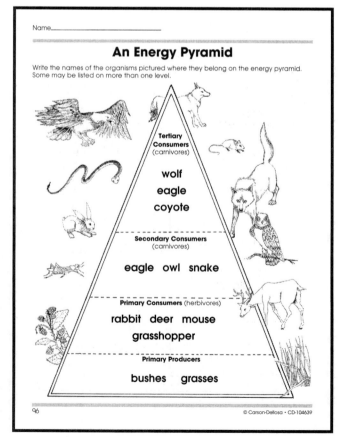

An Energy Pyramid

Write the names of the organisms pictured where they belong on the energy pyramid. Some may be listed on more than one level.

Tertiary Consumers (carnivores)
wolf
eagle
coyote

Secondary Consumers (carnivores)
eagle owl snake

Primary Consumers (herbivores)
rabbit deer mouse
grasshopper

Primary Producers
bushes grasses

96   © Carson-Dellosa • CD-104639

Answer Key

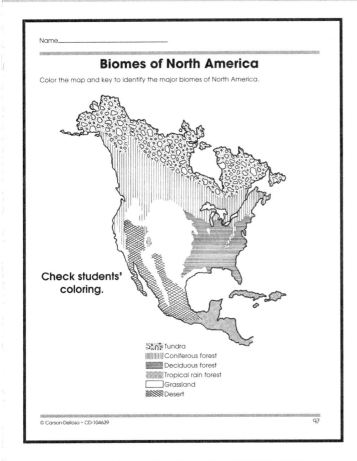
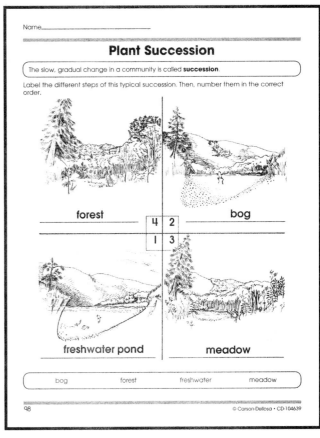
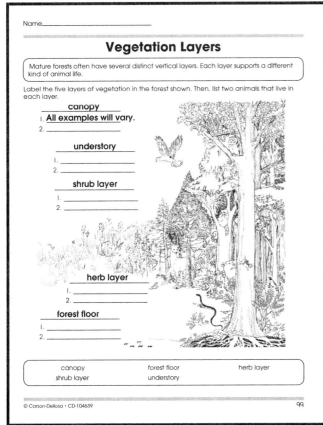
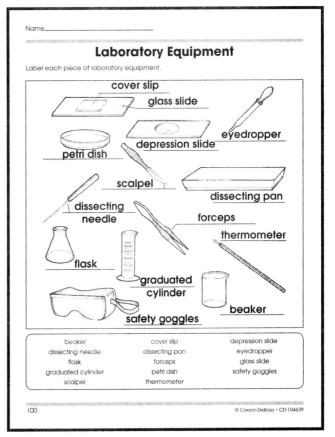

Answer Key

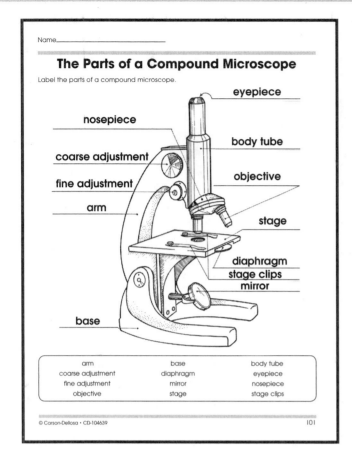

The Parts of a Compound Microscope

Label the parts of a compound microscope.

eyepiece

nosepiece

body tube

coarse adjustment

objective

fine adjustment

arm

stage

diaphragm
stage clips
mirror

base

arm	base	body tube
coarse adjustment	diaphragm	eyepiece
fine adjustment	mirror	nosepiece
objective	stage	stage clips

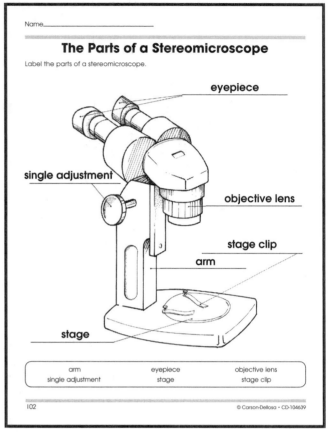

The Parts of a Stereomicroscope

Label the parts of a stereomicroscope.

eyepiece

single adjustment

objective lens

stage clip

arm

stage

arm	eyepiece	objective lens
single adjustment	stage	stage clip